WHAT LAWYERS DO:
A PROBLEM-SOLVING APPROACH
TO LEGAL PRACTICE

University of
Chester

Library

This book is to be returned on or before the last date stamped
below. Overdue charges will be incurred by the late return of
books.

AUSTRALIA
LBC Information Services
Sydney

CANADA and USA
Carswell
Toronto

NEW ZEALAND
Brooker's
Auckland

SINGAPORE and MALAYSIA
Thomson Information (S.E. Asia)
Singapore

WHAT LAWYERS DO: A PROBLEM-SOLVING APPROACH TO LEGAL PRACTICE

BY

STEPHEN NATHANSON

First Edition

London • Sweet & Maxwell • 1997

*Published in 1997 by Sweet & Maxwell Limited of
100 Avenue Road, Swiss Cottage
London NW3 3PF
Typeset by Tradespools Ltd,
Frome
Printed in England by Clays Ltd,
St Ives plc*

No Natural forests were destroyed to make this product;
only farmed timber was used and replanted

**A CIP catalogue record for this book is available from the British
Library**

ISBN 0421 548 908

To Ginger

CONTENTS

Preface

PREFACE

Not too long ago, legal education was far removed from the practice of law. Students in law schools learned contract, tort, criminal and property law as well as other 'core' subjects. These subjects covered legal rules and principles and the ways judges interpret them. Students learned from traditional teaching methods such as lectures, tutorials and Socratic questioning. What lawyers actually do rarely played a role in the curriculum, and students learned little about legal practice until after they graduated and went out into the real world.

Since then the quality of legal education has improved. Many undergraduate law schools have introduced courses in legal skills to teach the practice of law. In the United Kingdom and the Common-wealth, post-LL.B. professional courses have been designed to prepare students for practice. Teachers are also using more modern teaching and learning methods such as simulations, video demonstrations and feedback, distance learning, internet learning and systematically designed learning materials.

Despite these improvements, legal education still has some way to go in providing relevant learning experiences for law students. Holding back the development of legal education are two divergent outlooks pulling it in different directions: one outlook sees the purpose of legal education as teaching academic or theoretical law and the other as teaching legal practice. Through the years, these two outlooks have grown antagonistic to each other and points of reconciliation between them are hard to find. The result is that the providers of legal education have, by and large, been unable to agree on, or design, a set of integrated and meaningful learning experiences for students. Academic legal education seems unrelated to practice and legal-practice education seems to lack a strong theoretical framework: This book is an attempt to bring the two outlooks closer together by explaining how law relates to practice and how practice is based on theory and principles.

The idea for the book germinated years ago when I worked as one of the designers of the Professional Legal Training Course (PLTC) in British Columbia. PLTC was established to train LL.B. graduates, in-firm trainees, and lawyers from other jurisdictions to a level of competence that would qualify them for legal practice. The Law Society of British Columbia directed that the course, which was to be delivered in ten weeks, meet a wide variety of learning objectives. Because the period was short and the aim so ambitious, the design had to be highly efficient. And because PLTC was one of the first programmes of its kind, the designers had to work largely through trial and error. They had to organise diverse subjects, integrate skills and transactions, and select the most efficient teaching methods. They also had to work closely with the students, all of whom were post-graduates, and most of whom had law-office and courtroom experience. They were much more demanding about their learning needs than less experienced, undergraduate students.

In this high-pressure environment, some of the designers began to see the need for a simple, theoretical framework for the course. They searched for theories to tie together the various elements of the course to make it easier to grasp. They adapted and developed theories of skills such as interviewing, advocacy, drafting, writing and negotiation. They worked on weaving these skills together in coherent patterns. In addition, they searched for ways to integrate legal skills with the legal knowledge students learned as undergraduates and the professional attitudes they would need for practice. The designers soon discovered that one of the main objectives of the course was to strive to create a unifying theory of legal practice in order to provide both an organising principle for the course as a whole and a sound framework for students to help them conceptualise what lawyers do.

After I left PLTC and become involved in designing other legal-practice courses, I continued searching for a theory of legal practice. Eventually, I saw *problem solving* as the most logical choice. Problem solving was being used as a theme, if not an explicit theory, in many professional-education programmes including medicine, dentistry, nursing, management, business, engineering, architecture and law. This may have been because many teachers viewed the ability to solve difficult problems as one of the most important features of professional work. It was no accident that curricula in the professions were increasingly designed around this theme. To my way of thinking, defining competent lawyering as the ability to solve legal problems seemed to make the most sense from both a curriculum-design and a theoretical standpoint.

This book is the result of that thinking. It presents a theory of legal practice based on problem solving. It relates the knowledge and skills learned in law school with the problem-solving tasks lawyers perform in practice. It will help students develop a realistic perspective on what they are learning and provide them with a better understanding of legal practice as well as what it means to be a lawyer.

What Lawyers Do is written for an audience in all common law countries. Although specific references to law are mainly of English origin, examples of legal practice are drawn from Britain, Canada, the United States, Hong Kong, Australia and New Zealand. As a result, while writing the book I had a bit of a dilemma selecting appropriate legal terminology. To British readers, used to terms such as 'retaining a solicitor' or 'briefing counsel', 'hiring a lawyer' may be somewhat off-putting. To American readers, 'real-property conveyancing' may sound alien and 'fixed and floating charges' would undoubtedly be concepts many have never heard of. In the end, I decided simply to use terms that I believed had the widest application and presented the least ambiguity.

For helping me with this book, I would like to express my heartfelt gratitude to my wife, Ginger, who edited and reorganised material and suggested many new ideas and ways of looking at things.

I would also like to thank Raymond Wacks for his support and advice.

Credit should also go to Anne Carver who co-authored Chapter 1 and provided editing and research assistance.

Others who contributed to this book whom I would like to thank include Kelly Busche, Alison Conner, John Joseph, Kitty Lai, Shane Nossal, Maureen Sabine, Michael Sandor, Patsy Scheer, Magdalen Spooner, Tony Tobin, Rita Wai and Michael Wilkinson.

ACKNOWLEDGMENTS

Extract from Kurt Vonnegut, *God Bless You, Mr Rosewater*, reproduced by permission of Donald C. Farber, the Attorney for Kurt Vonnegut.

Extract from David Binder & Paul Bergman, *Fact Investigation: From Hypothesis to Proof*, (1984) reproduced with permission of the West Publishing Corporation, Minnesota.

Extract from *'Negotiation'*, in *Legal Ethics: Applying the Model Rules, Discussion Guides for the ABA Videolaw Seminar* (1984) is reprinted by permission of the American Bar Association and authors.

Extract from *Quackery and Contract Law: The case of the Carbolic Smokeball*, Journal of Legal Studies, Vol. XVI, June 1985, © 1985 by The University of Chicago.

Extract from *Adjudication and Interpretation in the Common Law*, Legal Studies (1994) No.1, reproduced with permission of Butterworths.

Extract from *The Dialogues of Plato*, translated by Benjamin Jowett into English from *Theuteyus*, 1973, reproduced with permission of Oxford University Press.

Extract from John Mortimer, *Rumpole and the Man of God (The Trials of Rumpole)*, reproduced with permission of the Peters Fraser & Dunlop Group Ltd.

Extract from Peter T. Burns, editor, and Susan J. Lyons, associate editor, *Donoghue v. Stevenson and the Modern Law of Negligence: The Paisley Papers, the Proceedings of the Paisley Conference on the Law of Negligence*, (1991), reproduced with permission of the editor.

Acknowledgment is made for the extracts from the following works:

Extract from John L. Jenkins, *The Litigators*, (St Martin's Paperback edition, 1991), Acton, Dystel, Leone and Jaffe, New York.

Extract from Charles Rembar, *The Law of the Land*, (1980), Simon & Schuster, New York.

Extract from Gerry Spence, *With Justice for None*, (1989), Times Books, a Division of Random House, New York.

Extract from *National*, Volume 18, No. 8, October, 1991, Ottawa.

Extract from C.H. Rolph, *The Trials of Lady Chatterley—Regina v. Penguin Books Ltd*, 1961.

CHAPTER 1

IMAGES OF THE LAWYER

This book is written for people who want to learn to be lawyers or want to know what lawyers do. Many people have inaccurate images of the roles played by lawyers, most of which are drawn from personal experience or exposure to literature and the media. Even students in law school may have only a hazy idea of what lawyers do. This lack of clarity often continues into later stages of their development when students are studying for professional or bar examinations, or just beginning legal practice.

Although it is true that the degree to which aspiring lawyers misconstrue what lawyers do varies from person to person, two common themes run through this misconception. The first is that students' ideas of what lawyers do is distorted by previous experience. The second is that students are unable to develop a realistic picture of what lawyers do from law school because most schools teach different aspects of law, not how to practise law.

Law students' misconception about what lawyers do begins before law school and becomes further distorted in law school. Law schools devote much of their resources to teaching students legal knowledge and ways of applying that knowledge in legal argument; they tend not to focus on teaching students how to solve clients' real-life legal problems. When students start law school, the tasks they are given are disconnected from the images they have of what lawyers do. This can be confusing for law students and can develop into serious difficulty later on when they attempt to integrate their legal education into legal practice.

Some law teachers have difficulty helping students see the relevance of what they are learning and where the tasks they are given fit into the scheme of things. Students are unsure, for example, where tasks such as case reading and analysis fit into the scheme of what a lawyer actually does. It is as if they have been given only one piece of a jigsaw puzzle without the other pieces and without a picture of the completed puzzle on the box.

When young lawyers begin to practise, they continue to have difficulty relating the tasks they are given to do, such as drafting documents, interviewing witnesses or writing letters, to what they have learned in law school. Often they are asked to do things as separate, unrelated activities, and it is hard for them to see the relationship between these tasks and the overall objective. It is true that young lawyers get more pieces of the puzzle than law students do, but they still do not get a complete picture of the overall objective.

The purpose of this book is to present a clear picture of what lawyers do not by giving tips on how to do specific legal tasks, but by identifying and exploring the essence of what it means to practise law competently. The basic premise of this book is that if students and new lawyers could see the big picture at the start, they would be able to fit the pieces together more easily later on. Understanding the big picture may well be the most useful first step one can take in learning how to be a lawyer. For people who have already started learning how to be one, or are practising law now, this book may help them put their ideas about what lawyers really do into perspective.

In this first chapter the exploration begins by examining some of the more popular *images* of the lawyer. Some of these images are negative and others positive; some aspects of them are realistic, some distorted. Nonetheless, these familiar images are a good starting point in the search for the lawyer's essence and, ultimately, in creating a clear and coherent picture of what lawyers do.

A GALLERY OF IMAGES

The lawyer as distorter of truth

Popularised in film and the media, the lawyer is seldom portrayed accurately. Because of this, people often misunderstand what lawyers do. One of the most misunderstood images of a lawyer is the role of advocate. To lay people, an effective advocate is a persuader, and a persuader is a manipulator and twister of the truth. Persuaders do not speak or seek the truth; they twist it in their favour in order to persuade. Persuaders are intelligent, but their intelligence is employed to manipulate people and events, rather than to dispense wisdom.

From the earliest times, critics of lawyers have regarded them with cynicism. In Plato's world, for instance, there was no place for the sophistry of lawyers. Plato exalted the search for truth and, in his eyes, lawyers were obstacles to that search. Plato's search was to be conducted through the dialectic, the philosopher's route to truth, not through legal argument.

> "[The lawyer] is a servant, and is continually disputing about a fellow-servant before his master, who is seated, and has the cause in his hands; the trial is never about some indifferent matter, but always concerns himself; and often the race is for his life. The consequence has been, that he has become keen and shrewd; he has learned how to

flatter his master in word and indulge him in deed; but his soul is small and unrighteous. His condition, which has been that of a slave from his youth upwards, has deprived him of growth and uprightness and independence; dangers and fears, which were too much for his truth and honesty, came upon him in early years, when the tenderness of youth was unequal to them, and he has been driven into crooked ways; from the first he has practised deception and retaliation, and has become stunted and warped. And so he has passed out of youth into manhood, has no soundness in him; and is now, as he thinks, a master in wisdom. Such is the lawyer, Theodorus."[1]

The view of the lawyer as distorter of truth is a common one even today, but it is a narrow view, revealing an incomplete understanding of the lawyer's role in the system. In the adversarial legal system, it is not the lawyer's role to give evidence, but the role of the witnesses. It is not the lawyer's role to find the truth, but the duty of the judge or jury. It is the lawyer's duty as an advocate to do the best for the client through the art of persuasion, which means presenting the evidence in the best possible light.

Lawyers should be able to be persuasive advocates without having to lie or misstate the evidence. Lawyers who do develop a reputation for lying or distorting will become known in the legal community and quickly lose their credibility with judges. Once lost, credibility is difficult to recover. Without credibility, the lawyer's arguments can lose their ethical appeal and this, in turn, can damage the effectiveness of the lawyer as a persuader. Generally speaking, lawyers abide by the rules of ethics in presenting their client's case. The image of the lawyer as a distorter of truth is undeserved.

The lawyer as paper generator

To ensure fairness, the adversarial system is rule-bound. Procedural requirements exist for every conceivable situation and they help to establish a level playing field. But shrewd lawyers know how to exploit the rules to delay proceedings, exhaust the financial resources of the opposition, or make things difficult by confusing the issues. One of the lawyer's tools for creating confusion is to generate paperwork.

A common image exists of the lawyer as paper generator, living off paperwork — creating, copying, analysing and organising reams of paper for no ostensible reason other than to complicate the simple or to inflate fees. Probably the most famous caricature of this image is Mr Tangle, the solicitor in Dickens' *Bleak House*, the only person who understands *Jarndyce v. Jarndyce*, an incomprehensible case that has been winding its way through the Chancery Courts for years. John Jarndyce, an unwilling party to the litigation, talks about all the lawyers involved in that famous case:

> "The lawyers have twisted it into such a state of bedevilment that the original merits of the case have long disappeared from the face of the earth. It's about a will, and the trusts under a will — or it was, once. We are always appearing and disappearing, and swearing and interrogating, and filing, and cross-filing, and arguing, and sealing and motioning, and referring, and reporting, and revolving about the Lord Chancellor and all his satellites, and equitably waltzing ourselves off to dusty death about costs. That's the great question. All the rest, by some extraordinary means has melted away."[2]

John Jarndyce goes on to describe the copying:

> "Everybody must have copies, over and over again, of everything that has accumulated about it in the way of cartloads of papers (or must pay for them without having them, which is the usual course for nobody wants them)."[3]

As with all great caricature, this portrayal has a grain of truth in it. The system and the prevailing rules require a great deal of paperwork. But it is not lawyers who insist on paperwork. In litigation, as in other areas of legal work, words on paper are the currency of practice. While a few lawyers may create more paperwork than necessary, competent lawyers do nothing more than draft, analyse and organise documents to meet their clients' goals. The image of lawyers and clients overwhelmed by a mountain of documents may be amusing, but it is inaccurate and should remain relegated to Victorian novels. Competent lawyers are not paper-pushers, and legal paperwork is not inherently wasteful. Drafting legal documents and handling them effectively are all part of what a competent lawyer does.

The lawyer as sorcerer

Legal documents are important not only in the work of advocates, but also in what non-advocate lawyers do. The non-advocate's image has run afoul of public opinion in much the same way as the advocate's image, and documents once again have played a prominent role in defaming the lawyer. When lay people are confronted with complicated documents filled with legal jargon it is easy for them to jump to conclusions and imagine lawyers playing tricks and devising fraudulent schemes. The seventeenth-century poet, John Donne, himself a lawyer, saw lawyers as a social disease because he thought they drafted legal documents for the purpose of cheating their own clients.[4] Chaucer seems to have held a similar view. In *The Canterbury Tales*, the Man of Law tricked his client by pretending to clear up legal problems in land titles by redrafting documents, when in reality he redrafted them in his own favour.[5]

To some lay people, lawyers may not necessarily be fraudulent, but they do appear to use incomprehensible language and ever lengthier documents to complicate the simple, justifying higher fees while submerging their real intentions in a sea of murky legal language. To these people, lawyers are sorcerers who use linguistic formulae in documents to win advantages for their clients. This last perception is probably closer to the mark than the others. Non-advocate lawyers use documents to advance their clients' interests. As we shall see in Chapter 7, the underlying purpose of many types of legal document is not to create difficulties, but to prevent them from occurring later, after the documents have been signed. Competent lawyers use documents not to satisfy their own needs, but to achieve their client's goals by preventing or *blocking* conflicts.

The lawyer as hero

In popular culture, images of the lawyer are not only villainous or amusing, but heroic. The lawyer is frequently portrayed as a truth-seeker and defender of the wrongly accused. This heroic image of the lawyer is appealing to law students who want to achieve great things in their lives through a legal career. The lawyer as hero is a contemporary knight who defends the oppressed with courage and moral conviction.

In Harper Lee's novel *To Kill A Mockingbird*, Atticus Finch is the reluctant hero/lawyer. Made into a film in 1962, *To Kill A Mockingbird*[6] is set in the American South. Gregory Peck plays the humble and dignified Atticus Finch, a lawyer who feels he must stand up for what is right. Finch is determined to defend Tom Robinson, a black man unjustly accused of raping and brutally assaulting a white farmer's daughter, Ella Mae Ewall, a girl who had enraged her father by kissing Tom Robinson in his presence.

In an atmosphere charged with racial tension, the trial proceeds. The evidence points to the fact that Ella Mae was assaulted by a left-handed person. Finch proves to the jury that Tom Robinson is right-handed. Finch cross-examines Ella Mae's father, and by asking him to write his name for the court, demonstrates he is left-handed. Through the cross-examination, the court is left with the impression that Ella Mae's father is the killer.

In his closing speech to the jury, Finch reiterates the motive of Ella Mae's father for killing her: she has broken the colour taboo by kissing Tom Robinson: "She is the victim of poverty and guilt. She has broken a time-honoured code of our society."

In his appeal to the jury, Finch describes how the courtroom should be a leveller between rich and poor, black and white. He tells the jury, "In the name of God, do your duty." The jury, however, would not allow the time-honoured code to be broken, and finds Tom Robinson guilty of the rape and assault. On being taken to Abbotsville Gaol for safety, Tom Robinson tries to escape and is killed by the Deputy Sheriff.

Finch is a classic hero/lawyer because he represented a wrongly accused black man in the Deep South. Although real lawyers seldom encounter this level of adversity, all lawyers, especially courtroom lawyers, have to uphold their client's interest with courage in the face of pressure, and sometimes hostility, from accusers, police, prosecution and judiciary.

The lawyer as hero, however, is a misleading image for aspiring lawyers. When thinking about what lawyers do, it is always helpful to focus on the client — in this case the innocent Tom Robinson. What Tom Robinson really wanted was to be acquitted of a crime he did not commit. Whether or not Finch behaved heroically in the process was beside the point.

Admittedly, Finch's job was difficult, but that is a predicament that could elicit sympathy for Finch only in an audience, not in clients. Clients such as Tom Robinson are not in a position to sympathise with the difficulties faced by their lawyers. For them it is results that count. They cannot afford to lose and they want their lawyers to use all their skills in solving the problem of how to win.

Perhaps Finch should have been less of a hero and more a student of how to win a case in grimly difficult circumstances. For example, when Finch said to the jury, "In the name of God, do your duty," some lawyers would say a remark like that displays incompetent courtroom practice: it is a challenge to a jury, and juries do not like challenges. When juries are challenged to do something, it often provokes them to do the opposite. Prejudiced, hostile juries are even less open to challenges of this sort. Skilfully communicating with the jury was, during the summation, more important than telling them what was morally right.

The lawyer as hero, like other lawyer images, can distract us from the essence of what a lawyer really does. Lawyers act for clients. What lawyers do must be evaluated according to their clients' needs. When clients hire lawyers to defend them, they need them to win, not to be heroes and lose.

The lawyer as underdog

Although winning for clients is an important element of the lawyer's job, it is by no means the only element. If lawyers focus only on winning and neglect the client's wider concerns, real damage can be done. This, however, is a subtle point that may have been lost on the screenwriters who wrote *The Verdict*. As with all screenwriters, they wanted to ensure the audience identified with the main character. Since film audiences love underdogs who come from behind to win, why not portray the lawyer as underdog, or as outright loser, who redeems himself by coming from behind to win against superior forces and even his own character flaws? This may have been the screenwriters' reasoning when they put *The Verdict* together.

In *The Verdict*,[7] Paul Newman plays a down-and-out, heavy-drinking, self-pitying lawyer named Frank Galvin. Galvin represents Deborah Anne Kay in a negligence suit against a hospital and the doctors who operated on her. Acting for the hospital and doctors is the urbane and successful Ed Kilcannon, played by James Mason. Kilcannon's enormous law firm has the resources to provide him with 12 associates working round the clock to prepare the case for the defence.

Complicating this David-and-Goliath scenario is the fact that the family of Deborah Anne, who was left comatose by her treatment in the hospital, wants to settle. The defendants' insurers have just offered a lump sum payment of $210,000 with 30 per cent of that figure going to the lawyer.

Galvin visits Deborah Anne in the hospital, and while photographing her, achieves an insight that may be unremarkable to the audience, but is an eye-opener to him: Deborah Anne is not merely a source of income to a personal injury lawyer; she is actually a human being, a helpless victim of wrongdoing. He resolves to stand up for her rights. Instead of accepting the offered settlement, he decides to proceed to court against the wishes of Deborah Anne's family.

Alone and newly sober, Galvin fights to demonstrate to the jury that the facts of the case prove negligence and that the jury should find in favour of his client. Against all odds, and highlighted by a melodramatic address to the jury, he succeeds.

Unexplored in *The Verdict* is both the ethical issue of ignoring the family's instructions and Galvin's own negligence in going to trial without carefully reviewing all the options and the risks. Even if the family were not in a legal position to instruct Galvin on behalf of

Deborah Anne, what entitled him to ignore the family's wishes? He
should have consulted them and Deborah Anne's trustees. He should
have fully explored the options and the risks with them. For example, it
may have been possible to try to gather more evidence, or to engage in
new tactics to get Kilcannon to increase his offer. If Kilcannon had so
many more litigation resources to fight with, was there any way Galvin
and the family could have agreed on how to increase their own
resources? Given the meagre resources Galvin did have, and the
evidence available, what was the probability of his getting a better result
from the jury than Kilcannon was offering? And suppose Galvin had
lost? None of these issues was explored.

Also not explained was why Galvin was hired in the first place.
Clients generally do not want underdogs for lawyers, particularly ones
that drink heavily and are emotionally unstable. They want people who
are in control and able to provide them with the benefit of their good
judgment. The last thing clients want is for their lawyers to be making
decisions on the basis of what gives their lawyers the greatest possible
gratification — even if they do look like Paul Newman. The most
misleading aspect of this image of a lawyer as underdog is that it
overlooks the importance of competent decision-making in law practice.
It is safe to conclude that the underdog/lawyer is as useful to clients as
the hero/lawyer.

The lawyer as dramatic character

Less misleading and more realistic, the images presented by the lawyers
in the television series *L.A. Law*[8] were as varied as the situations in
which they found themselves. Unlike many of Hollywood's heroes,
their professional lives and the decisions they were called upon to make
were not ruled by simplistic themes. Sometimes they made the wrong
decisions. Sometimes they lost cases. They often negotiated and settled
them; they fired clients and were fired in turn; they misbehaved and
agonised over ethical dilemmas. Practising law for *L.A. Law*'s lawyers
was complicated by realistic problems that often had no clear-cut
answers.

L.A. Law was so popular that the dramatic characters in it were
accepted as real people with practical concerns who just happened to be
rich and beautiful. Nevertheless, it was this tendency to portray lawyers
as real people with real concerns that, ironically, led the audience astray
in its understanding of what real lawyers do. This is because the series
was less focused on lawyers than it was on people who are engaged in a
dramatic search for who they really are. For much of the time, the search
was played out in the context of their work under pressure of office

politics, ethical dilemmas, or legal disputes. In a span of 50 minutes, conflicts were resolved and insights gained. The lawyers in *L.A. Law* fought for the underdog, made lots of money, but also learned who they were and who they should be in a weekly dramatisation filled with well-timed insights.

This dramatic image of the lawyer can be confusing for people trying to understand what lawyers really do, because the image focuses more on the lawyer doing things to satisfy his or her own needs rather than the client's needs. Although this emphasis made the show entertaining and enabled the audience to identify with the lawyers, the portrayal of what lawyers do is, for this reason, frequently off the mark.

To understand what lawyers do, it is better to focus on how lawyers solve their clients' problems, not their own. Like Tom Robinson in *To Kill A Mockingbird*, clients are unconcerned with their lawyers' personal problems. They want their lawyers to deal with *their* problems. This is what they are paying for.

The dramatic-character image is also unrealistic because it places too much emphasis on how easy it is to be everything — lawyer fighting for the underdog, lawyer making lots of money, lawyer gaining new insights every week. The tough aspects of being a lawyer were left out of *L.A. Law* — lawyer consumed by detail and documents, lawyer weighed down by a sense of responsibility towards client, lawyer applying all available knowledge and skills to demanding problems. These and other aspects of lawyers' work were not portrayed because they do little to create dramatic effect. After all, *L.A. Law* was dramatic entertainment and the programme's aim was to entertain. *L.A. Law* was more about a group of people living dramatic lives who happen to be lawyers, than about what lawyers really do.

The lawyer as saviour

In the early stages of American television, 1957 to 1965, Raymond Burr created one of the best known images of the lawyer. He played the defence attorney, Perry Mason.[9] Mason, whose clients were always completely innocent, never lost a case. Perry Mason's penetrating eyes, detached concern for his clients, unwavering search for the truth and relentless cross-examination of the culprit, combined to immortalise an image which gave us the lawyer as saviour.

Of course, the *Perry Mason* series was a formulaic whodunnit with few pretensions to realism. Real clients charged with criminal offences are not usually innocent. Real defence lawyers are not supposed to search for the truth. Searching for the truth is the prosecution's duty, not that of the defence. Real witnesses rarely break down in court and confess their guilt on cross-examination. Nevertheless, the most salient feature of this blatant unreality was the degree to which it was ignored by viewers. Each week, thousands of them wrote to Raymond Burr seeking legal advice. Even lawyers, who were supposed to know better, admired Perry Mason. They frequently invited Raymond Burr, who was an actor not a lawyer, to address legal gatherings. Why they admired him had little to do with his legal skills. He simply made them look good. He was good for their image.

Though unrealistic, Perry Mason did display characteristics that are instructive, not so much about what lawyers really do, but about the *attitudes* lawyers should adopt to engender confidence in their clients. Clients had confidence in Perry Mason, not just because he always won, but because he appeared to be completely focused on his job. He had no other concerns and no other cases. He never became emotionally involved with his clients (or indeed with anything or anybody). He remained objective, calm and sympathetic. Unlike *L.A. Law*'s lawyers, Perry Mason never went through the process of learning about himself; if he had, it would have struck his audience as an unpardonable egotistical lapse. He never had any insights about himself or about the mysteries of life. His only insights were in relation to how he could prove his client's innocence. He was so uninterested in himself and his own needs, he never even fell in love. Only occasionally did he allow himself the indulgence of flirting and that was with Della Street, his faithful secretary. But even these flirtations were ambiguous, and could be interpreted as tokens of appreciation for her long hours. Perry Mason had no personal life whatsoever. His whole life was dedicated to saving his clients.

For clients, having a lawyer as dedicated and selfless as Perry Mason may be an unrealistic expectation but still a common fantasy, especially for those in trouble with the law. The image of lawyer as saviour may be unreal, but it is an image that gives great comfort and confidence to clients. As such, though it may never be realised, it is still an image to which lawyers should aspire.

The lawyer as warrior

On British television, John Mortimer's Horace Rumpole[10] also defends the accused. Rumpole's clients are not always guiltless, but they are portrayed as underdogs, nonetheless. Unlike his American counterparts, Rumpole does not enjoy lucrative fees, stylish suits and a sleek, youthful appearance. He is an old, fat crumpled barrister who fights for people, some of whom do not even deserve his dedication. His personal life is depressing. He drinks too much, is by-passed for honours by younger, more polished barristers, and suffers from a cheerless marriage to a wife he refers to as "she who must be obeyed".[11]

Rumpole specialises in small-time criminal work in the Old Bailey. Part of the appeal of both the stories and the television series is in Rumpole's crusade for the little man against establishment judges and their allies, the police. Rumpole believes that while the dice are loaded against his seedy clients, the rule of law embodied in the common law system which he passionately maintains will ultimately prevail, thus giving the underclass a fighting chance.

Rumpole is opinionated, cunning and antagonistic. He does not like many of the people who inhabit the legal system — particularly the judges and opposing counsel. His dislike of these people is often laced with antagonism toward the upper classes to which these people belong or try to belong. But whatever their class or their accent, Rumpole would probably regard them as his enemy anyway. To Rumpole, practising law is war.

It is this warrior-like stance, together with his profound respect for and understanding of the legal system, that makes Rumpole so unique, yet so real as an advocate; he distrusts and dislikes people, but loves the system. In a shoplifting trial, before Judge Bullingham, whom Rumpole calls "the Bull," he does a cross-examination of a store detective that plays on the English jury's natural distaste for shop assistants. Through brilliant cross-examination Rumpole constructs a defence based on the unhelpfulness of shop assistants who are too busy gossiping to take his client's money. "It's a risky business entering your store isn't it?" Rumpole puts it to the store detective in a mocking tone. "You can't get served and no-one speaks to you except to tell you that you are under arrest".[12]

During the cross-examination, the Bull interrupts Rumpole several times, but Rumpole cleverly manipulates the interruptions, making his rejoinders more to the jury than the judge so he can score points for his client. He is hostile and sarcastic, but never crosses over to the realm of insult or contempt of court. He is in verbal combat right until the end when, after the prosecution has presented its evidence, he argues that there is no case to answer because the evidence failed to show his client intended to shoplift. He asks the judge to direct the jury to acquit his client. When the Bull acquiesces, Rumpole tells the reader, "The natural malice of the Bull had been quelled by his instinctive respect for the law."[13]

In the end, it is unclear whether Rumpole hates the judge and the prosecutor personally, or dislikes them for the roles they play. Whether it is personal or not, Rumpole works in an adversarial system and knows he will not gain any points for liking or trusting his adversaries. In

Rumpole's world, only the legal system and the law can be relied on. The law is regarded as almost a divine force, something that even detestable people cannot fail to respect. It may be burdened with old-fashioned traditions such as medieval chambers, bewigged barristers and arcane legal language, but Rumpole knows how to mediate between his clients and the system. He uses all his considerable skills, backed up by a ferocious, but consistently effective, style to squeeze the best out of it for the benefit of his clients.

Listening to Rumpole you can sense his total dedication to his clients not because he feels sympathy for their unfortunate predicaments, but because you can see how much energy, thought and skill he has invested in his courtroom strategies. Like Perry Mason, he is utterly absorbed in the problem of how to help his clients. But the problems Rumpole deals with and the strategies for solving them are usually more realistic; most of the time, Rumpole is able to select and put into practice strategies appropriate to those problems. Unlike *L.A. Law*'s lawyers he has few personal indulgences except for his drinking and hostile asides. His fans know that these antics are all part of his character which, of course, are put to good use in his work.

In many ways, Rumpole is right to regard courtroom practice as a form of war. It is a war clients want their lawyers to win, and a certain degree of aggression and distrust, if properly channelled, keeps the warrior and his weapons well-honed. Good advocates enjoy fighting.

Gerry Spence, the American trial lawyer, expresses similar views about the advocate's role. To him, a trial is a fight and the "maiming is done with words."[14] Trial lawyers are fighters "struggling to accomplish justice under the great disability of a legal education."[15] In his showy account of his life in America's courtrooms, *With Justice For None*, he says:

> "I train for a trial, run in order to be physically fit, eat right, and sleep right. To prepare mentally for it, I concentrate on the justice of my client's case, on my anger... Anger is the fuel of the fight, the life force of the trial... In the courtroom, my opponents feel my anger, know my physical presence, and sense my commitment to my case; as the trial stretches into weeks, perhaps months, they learn that that anger continually replenishes the energy for battle and the will for victory."[16]

If trial work is war, then it stands to reason that the only thing that counts is winning. All one's knowledge, skills and personal qualities must be focused on this objective. According to Mr Spence, to win you should be able to be angry and feel angry. If Rumpole's personal qualities include ever-simmering, anti-establishment anger, then this quality, which is regarded by some as rather unattractive, may make him ideally suited to his profession.

And ideally suited he is, for Rumpole lives and breathes the law, being completely dedicated to the profession and the legal system. This immersion in the system complements his immersion in his client's problems. He is constantly thinking about and analysing both — to the ultimate benefit of his clients. Though some people may find Rumpole hard to take, with his sarcastic asides against wives, judges and others, his skill and dedication make his warrior-like image one of the few that is realistic and powerful enough to convey what a lawyer really does when it is being done well.

WHAT LAWYERS DO: CONTINUING THE SEARCH

The image of Horace Rumpole does not encapsulate the entire essence of what competent lawyers do. But this image is perhaps more accurate than many of the others because it is focused on clients' problems. Moreover, Rumpole's ferocity gives us an inkling of the degree of enthusiasm and dedication necessary to attack these problems success-fully. Understanding what lawyers do must begin with an understanding of what their clients really need and what kinds of attitudes in lawyers help to ensure those needs are met.

Other images, however, which are less well-known and less colourful could, if properly illuminated and blended together, give us a better idea of what they do. One obvious, under-represented image in the gallery of images described in this chapter is the lawyer who never sets foot inside the courtroom. Most of the lawyers discussed here are advocates or courtroom lawyers. In fact, most lawyers are not advocates. They do not argue cases before judges and even fewer of them argue cases before juries. The non-advocate lawyer who handles client problems and paperwork suffers from a different kind of image problem: a non-image problem. Most people are not familiar with what they do at all.

In the search for what the lawyer really does both types of lawyer and the relationship between the two will be examined. Even the terms advocate and non-advocate are misleading because both types of lawyer are advocates of one kind or another. They advocate their clients' interests, although they do it in different ways. The advocate/warrior is part of a broader category of lawyers that meets clients' goals by playing out conflict in order to win or resolve it peacefully. These *conflict-players* are the ones with whom the public is most familiar. The lawyers whom the public does not know as well are the *conflict-blockers*. These are lawyers who meet clients' goals by designing documents and procedures to prevent or *block* conflict.

Some people argue that the best place to start in learning how to be either type of lawyer is to learn about legal concepts, a subject that all lawyers should know something about. But being a competent lawyer involves a lot more than understanding legal concepts. Lawyers need to meet a variety of educational requirements and should have a good idea at the start what those requirements are. The next chapter explains *lawyering concepts* — the knowledge, skills and attitudes lawyers need to be competent.

[1] *The Dialogues of Plato*, translated into English by B. Jowett (Random House, New York 1973), "Theuteyus", p.175.

[2] Charles Dickens, *Bleak House*, Chapter VIII, cited in *The Dickens Dictionary* (William Clowes & Sons, London 1878), p.365.

[3] *ibid.*

[4] See, *e.g.* John Donne, "Satyre II", lines 62 and 64 in *The Complete Poetry and Selected Prose of John Donne*, ed. Charles M. Coffin (The Modern Library, New York, 1952), p.94.

[5] Geoffrey Chaucer, "The Man of Laws" in the *Canterbury Tales*. See, for example, F.N. Robinson, *The Works of Geoffrey Chaucer* (Oxford University Press, London, 2nd ed., 1957), p.3.

[6] *To Kill a Mockingbird* (Pakula-Mulligan Productions, CIC Video, c.1962), directed by Robert Mulligan 1962, adapted from the novel by Harper Lee.

[7] *The Verdict* (Twentieth Century Fox, New York. CBS/Fox Video, c.1982), directed by Sidney Lumet 1982, adapted from the novel by Barry Reed.

[8] *L.A. Law*, (NBC, 1986–1994).

[9] Perry Mason (CBS/Paisano, 1957–1965).

[10] John Mortimer's stories about the barrister Horace Rumpole, in *Rumpole of the Bailey* (1978), *The Trials of Rumpole* (1979), and *Rumpole's Return* (1983), (Penguin Books, Middlesex) were adapted into a British television series, *Rumpole of the Bailey* (Thames Television, Irene Shubik, 1978–1983).

[11] John Mortimer, "Rumpole and the Man of God", *The Trials of Rumpole in The First Omnibus* (Penguin Books, Middlesex, 1983), p.227.

[12] *ibid.*, p.226.

[13] *ibid.*, p.230.

[14] Gerry Spence, *With Justice for None* (Times Books, New York 1989), p.43.

[15] *ibid.*

[16] *ibid.*

CHAPTER 2

LAWYERING CONCEPTS

LEGAL CONCEPTS

In learning law, law students are introduced to a wide variety of legal concepts. They learn, for example, about the common law system, and how it is based not on legislation but on custom and the decisions of courts that interpret custom. They learn about legal concepts related to the common law system and how these developed in response to historical change. For example, the concept of equity with all its intricate legal fictions was developed through the centuries to fill a need in the English legal system. When the common law was incomplete or too inflexible the Court of Chancery was empowered to apply equitable rules in order to achieve just solutions.

Law students learn broad categories of concepts, such as substantive and procedural law. Substantive law consists of the rights people have and the obligations imposed on them. Procedural law governs the steps lawyers take to enforce a right clients want to exercise or protect. This may lead to a remedy, which is a form of justice one might seek from a court in compensation for a wrong that has been done. They learn that criminal law governs the relationship between the state and those accused of committing wrongs against it. It defines those wrongs and prescribes penalties for them. Civil law, on the other hand, is concerned with dealings between private individuals, defining their rights and obligations to each other and laying down methods for settling conflicts between them.

They also learn subjects such as contract and torts, which are organised groupings of related legal concepts. A contract is a binding exchange of promises and a breach of contract occurs when one or more of these is wrongly broken. A tort is a wrong that somebody commits when non-contractual duties are breached.

These and many other legal concepts are useful in describing and classifying law, in creating a systematically-organised body of knowledge with all its exceptions and in illustrating how different legal concepts are interrelated. They enable lawyers and judges to share the same vocabulary so that they can communicate with each other.

LAWYERING CONCEPTS

Although legal concepts have developed over hundreds of years, lawyering concepts are relatively new. To explain what lawyers do, it would be useful to know what lawyering concepts are and to have a vocabulary to describe them. Two notable research projects have been completed in this area. In 1991 Kim Economides and Jeff Smallcombe, on behalf of the Law Society of England and Wales, researched the knowledge, skills and attitudes needed by trainee solicitors and reported their findings in a report called *Preparatory Skills Training For Trainee Solicitors*.[1] In 1992 in America, the MacCrate Report, commissioned by the American Bar Association, made an effort to describe what it calls "Fundamental Lawyering Skills and Values" needed by lawyers before they can competently represent, or give advice to, clients.[2]

Both studies used a task-analysis approach to define what competent lawyers do. The researchers looked at lawyers' tasks and broke them down into lists of sub-tasks, skills, knowledge, personal attributes and other categories and sub-categories. Although this research advanced understanding of what lawyers do, from an educational standpoint it does present difficulty: because researchers do not want to omit important aspects of what lawyers do, the lists they make tend to be long, detailed and difficult for students to digest.

Knowing what it takes to be a competent lawyer is easier to understand when it includes two or three concepts rather than 50. When students are just beginning to learn a complicated assortment of skills such as how to be a lawyer, it makes sense for them to think about the skills in broad conceptual terms rather than to analyse them into a multitude of specific ones. With too much detailed analysis, it is easy to lose sight of the lawyering process as a whole.

Consider, for example, the doctoring process. For most people, understanding the essence of doctoring is easier than that of lawyering because most of us have been attended by doctors since birth. From the patient's viewpoint we know what they do, or we at least think we have a good idea. What do we think makes a competent general practitioner? I have compiled a list of five requirements based on my own experience:

A competent general practitioner is someone who:

(1) has a wide range of scientific and practical medical information and is familiar with a wide variety of ailments and treatments;
(2) is able to diagnose medical problems;
(3) is skilled in basic examination, treatment and other procedures;
(4) listens carefully;
(5) has concern for the patient's health or appears to.

Figure 2-1

These five requirements fall under three important categories: knowledge, skills and attitudes. The first requirement consists mainly of knowledge. The second and third requirements consist of knowledge and skills. The fourth requirement consists of skills and attitudes. And the fifth requirement consists mainly of attitudes. A competent general practitioner has to have a combination of knowledge, skills and attitudes. You would not want a doctor who has a concerned attitude, but cannot diagnose your problem, or one who seems extremely knowledgeable but does not listen, or one who skilfully uses procedures that you do not need.

The same goes for all professionals, including lawyers. All lawyers need the right blend of knowledge, skills and attitudes to be competent. What the precise formula should be, however, is debatable. Lawyers have varying opinions about what it takes to be a competent or even an excellent lawyer. And since lawyers do so many different kinds of things and have so many different specialities, it would be a waste of time to outline requirements about what lawyers need that are too specific and therefore unlikely to apply to a large number of lawyers. Nevertheless, it would be still be helpful to know generally what kind of knowledge, skills and attitudes lawyers need so that both educators and students can identify legal-education requirements.

This chapter and Figure 2-2 below present a model of the knowledge, skills and attitudes students need to be competent lawyers. With this information, students should be able to develop clearer educational goals and identify what they have to learn in order to become competent. It should also help them to put what they learn in law school in perspective. Called an *aggregate* model, it identifies and classifies a set of educational requirements for competence.

The Aggregate Model of Lawyer Competence

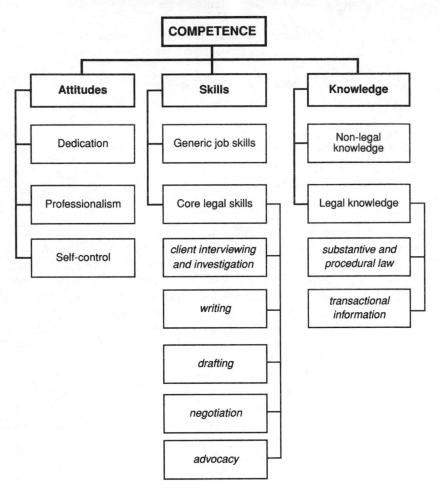

Figure 2-2

1. Attitudes

It is best to begin with attitudes, not because they are the most important (although they may well be), but because they are the simplest to understand and possibly the hardest to acquire. Attitudes are dispositions that influence people to behave in a certain way. Three particular attitudes are critical to competent practice: dedication, professionalism and self-control.

Dedication

The most basic attitude lawyers need is the same as for all professionals: enthusiasm for, and dedication to, the work. If lawyers do not like their work and are not dedicated to it, their capacity to persevere with difficult problems will be diminished, their ability to learn new things will be impaired and what they do day to day will be devoid of meaning. The need for dedication, hard work, attention to detail, and complete absorption in the problem at hand emerges not only in stories about lawyers such as Rumpole and Perry Mason, but is echoed again and again in the words of advice given by experienced lawyers. A young Canadian criminal defence lawyer, Ian Donaldson, who had already won many high-profile cases by the age of 34, explained his success in a newspaper interview:

"...there is no substitute for time. No matter how experienced you are, you cannot just look at a problem and snap onto a solution. It's a matter of hard work and being diligent. The more diligent you are, the more likely it is you will find flaws in a case that may have earlier been missed."[3]

While dedication is critical, it is advisable not to emulate Perry Mason completely. It is better to be able to switch one's mind off law sometimes and engage happily in pursuits outside it. Even so, there is no escape from the devotion needed for the job. Law is therefore something that students should want to do and feel good about, not something they have decided to do after eliminating other possibilities.

Professionalism

Part of being a professional is to maintain a professional stance towards clients and problems. This means being emotionally neutral and personally detached, irrespective of the clients' age, race, sex, religion, status or their personal history, including what they are alleged to have done.[4] The lawyer is not there to manipulate or judge clients, but to advise them, calmly and objectively, in their best interests.

Social pressure on lawyers to judge or dislike clients can be strong. For example, if the client has been charged with a terrible crime, it is easy to feel distaste for the client, particularly when the police and prosecution make their revulsion known. A young lawyer, sensitive to disapproval, can be susceptible to pressure applied by the authorities. This can influence his or her perception of the client's innocence. Policemen, in particular, are known to pack courtrooms, stare disapprovingly at counsel for the accused, and make casual remarks in the corridors during breaks to demonstrate how indignant they feel that such a desperado is actually pleading not guilty: "How can you sleep at night, knowing he might be acquitted because of you?", or "I hope you can get through this with a clear conscience!" Remarks such as these are heard not only in the dialogues of television cop shows; they reverberate in real-life courthouses and police stations.

Lawyers must resist these pressures, sometimes with courage, in order to maintain their professional stance and fulfil their duty to serve their clients' best interests. Lawyers have rules of conduct called Codes of Ethics that implicitly recognise these pressures and prescribe ways of dealing with them so that the lawyer's professional stance is preserved. One of the English Bar Code's best known ethical rules is that "a barrister has a duty to uphold the interests of his client without regard to his own interests or to any consequences to himself or to any other person."[5] This is an important rule that lawyers need to repeat to themselves when society expresses disapproval of their actions taken on behalf of clients.

Self-control

Since lawyers perform services for fees, and their financial interests do not always coincide with what their clients need, the pressure of self-interest can prevent lawyers from properly carrying out their duties. For example, lawyers sometimes get into situations where they act for more than one client in the same transaction when those clients may have opposing interests and may require conflicting advice; the temptation to multiply their fees can become too strong for some lawyers. Lawyers are also known to become involved with clients in business and play conflicting roles, both giving clients legal advice and doing business with them.

One of the most common accusations against lawyers in conflict-of-interest situations is that they overcomplicate transactions or drag out litigation in order to inflate their fees. While this sort of thing undoubtedly occurs, especially with wealthy, unwitting clients, nowadays clients are becoming more sophisticated about legal services, better able to detect make-work legal projects and bill-padding, and more disposed to complain to professional associations or change lawyers when not satisfied.

The conflict between client and lawyer interest is manifested in other ways. Rather than overcomplicate legal tasks in order to inflate their bills, what some lawyers do is to oversimplify them in order to conserve their own resources. For example, rather than doing all necessary investigations before completing a transaction they might omit a few, just to save time. Sometimes they do the opposite of dragging out litigation; they cut it short, settling cases quickly for less, so that they can improve their cash flow.

Another form of conflict is between the lawyer's duty to uphold the law and the need to win. As explained earlier, clients need to win. So for litigators, the pressure to win is intense. As one American litigator said about his firm:

"We just do litigation. And while we have one or two clients that we've done repeated lawsuits for, you could name on one hand the clients we can expect repeat business from. Our clients may never have the same problem again. The only way you can attract clients on that basis is to keep winning lawsuits. If you begin losing lawsuits, word gets out just as quickly that you are a loser as it got out that you were a winner.[6]

But lawyers cannot use any tactic to win; their conduct is circumscribed by ethical rules. They cannot deliberately put forward perjured evidence, lie to the court, or destroy evidence. The pressure to win, however, can make it tempting for lawyers to bend the rules. In New Zealand, a lawyer defending a client in a traffic-offence prosecution found someone who looked just like his client. He sat this "ringer" in the courtroom, talked to her in plain sight of the police, and tricked them into identifying her, rather than his client, as the offender.[7] The New Zealand Law Society took a dim view of this, citing him for unprofessional conduct for deliberately misleading the court.

The temptation to yield to unprofessional practices is ever present. Perhaps the best way to resist it is to learn to recognise and understand ethical problems as they arise and carefully control responses to them. Learning how to stick to ethical principles on a day-to-day basis means learning self-control.

Attitudes are the simplest aspect of lawyering to understand, but the most difficult to learn, because they are related to the values and beliefs we were brought up with and have developed over a long time. We learn values and beliefs from significant people such as parents, siblings and teachers, and from life experience. We frequently emulate the attitudes of others when we see that the way they act has led to success. In organisations such as law firms, senior people act as influential role models for those more junior and it is common to see the juniors adopt modes of dress, conduct and attitudes similar to their bosses.[8] It is easy to take on the values and beliefs of influential people with whom we work. Learning the wrong value can occur simply by wanting to emulate the wrong model. This can detrimentally affect the attitude of an individual. Perhaps the most successful strategy for acquiring professional attitudes is to identify and study those people who exhibit traits of dedication, professionalism and self-control.

2. Skills

"Generic job" skills and "Core legal" skills

To be competent, lawyers need to have skills. These skills are divided into two types, *generic job* skills and *legal* skills. Generic job skills are capabilities required in a variety of professions, including law. Generic job skills such as the ability to listen, question, communicate, organise, research, analyse, synthesise, plan, manage and handle money or computers effectively are all widely applied in professions that require higher-level capabilities.

Generic job skills can become *legal* skills when they are used to solve legal problems. The ability to question effectively is a generic job skill, but if the questioning is driven by legal knowledge, it takes on the colour of a legal skill. Similarly, research skills become legal-research skills when legal knowledge is added to the mix. Thus it can be said that all of the generic job skills may be regarded as legal skills when they are driven by legal knowledge or when they are used to solve legal problems. It is helpful also to regard all these *legal* skills as *component* skills, or parts of, more complex legal skills. For example, listening, questioning, communicating, researching, analysing, synthesising and planning are all component skills, or parts of, negotiation. Communicating, analysing, synthesising, researching and planning are all component skills of drafting.

Lawyers and law teachers have spent much time and effort trying to identify components of complex skills in order to define precisely the skills lawyers need to practice competently. They have even debated about which skills are generic and which are legal. To make matters more complicated, "legal skills" are sometimes called "generic" or "transferable" legal skills, because they can be used in, or "transferred" to, different legal transactions. For instance, advocacy skills can be transferred from a civil to a criminal trial. Negotiation skills can be transferred from a personal injury case to a commercial conflict.

Despite the confusion, the lesson to be learned from these attempts to identify component skills is invaluable. It helps students see the similarities among, and relationships between, different lawyers' skills. This in turn helps them learn skills more efficiently. If *listening* is a component skill of complex legal skills such as interviewing, advocacy and negotiation, students' listening skill can improve rapidly when the importance of listening is drawn to their attention in each of those three skills activities.

Fortunately, in recent years, the emphasis on comprehensive and systematic identification of components has faded, not because definitions of particular skills have become any clearer, but because many law teachers and lawyers have realised that precise definitions are not as important as reaching a consensus about which legal skills are worth teaching. That consensus seems to have focused on five major complex skills which themselves are comprised of some or all of the component legal skills. These complex skills are not only vital to practice, and commonly used by lawyers, but are highly transferable and useful to students in a variety of transactions. They have also gained broad acceptance in law schools and post-LL.B professional courses. Together they form what are called *The Core Legal Skills* essential to competent practice.

The Core Legal Skills

Figure 2-3

1. Client interviewing and investigation

Interviewing involves the skill of eliciting information from, and interacting with, clients to help them solve problems.[9] It consists of two basic stages: first, eliciting information through listening and questioning, and secondly, advising the client. The interview is often the first interaction the client has with the lawyer, so it is important for the lawyer to use this opportunity to build trust and confidence through interpersonal and technical skills. Interpersonal, or *soft*, skills are needed to establish rapport, especially in the first stage to find out what the client really needs and elicit relevant information. In the second stage of the interview, advising, technical skills are probably more important. Technical skills depend on legal knowledge and judgment learned from practical experience. They aid the process of identifying options, analysing their consequences and helping the client make a decision.

The reason interviewing has been combined with investigation is that in practice they are usually intertwined. In order to solve the client's problem as a whole, the lawyer must investigate the facts during the interview, and afterwards as well. After the interview, for example, the conflict player (or litigation lawyer) can scrutinise relevant documents and other evidence relating to the legal conflict. The conflict blocker (the lawyer who put deals together) can conduct investigations to ascertain if the assets the client is buying are properly valued.

2. Writing

Clear, persuasive, well-organised written communication is essential to competent practice. For clients trying to resolve a difficult conflict or to complete a transaction, a well-written letter of advice which summarises the key facts, applicable law, and an analysis of options, can set them on a path of rational decision-making. In a negotiation, an offer letter that has been persuasively written can have a powerful effect on the recipient. Writing is both a core legal skill, and a component skill of other core legal skills such as negotiation, drafting and advocacy.

3. Drafting

Although good writing is obviously a component skill of good drafting, it is useful to differentiate drafting from writing. The skill of writing is normally associated with informal documents such as letters and memoranda. Drafting, however, is associated with formal documents usually intended to create legal relations or to persuade. According to Robert Dick, drafting documents intended to create legal relations,

> "is legal thinking made visible. This visible legal thinking is to precipitate legal rights, duties, privileges and functions in definitive form. It is the formulation and preparation of legal documents such as deeds, contracts, leases, wills and trust agreements. In effect, preparing legal documents is like drafting statutes between the parties, setting out relationships and ground rules in codified form."[10]

Drafting of this type involves the creation of formal legal documents, usually based on precedents because these contain provisions that have been successfully tested in, or are designed to prevent, litigation. In short, they prevent or block conflict. A lawyer can work on improving the conflict-blocking aspects of formal documents by skilfully modifying precedents.[11]

Somewhere between drafting and writing is the skill of producing formal documents that do not seek to create legal relations, but to persuade. These are documents such as pleadings or affidavits that are a

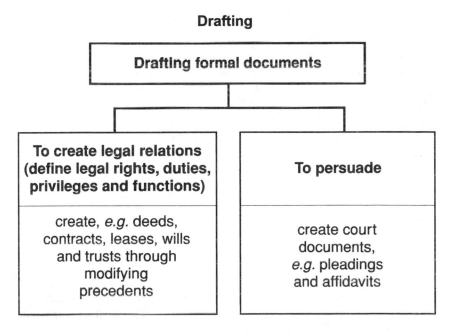

Drafting

Drafting formal documents	
To create legal relations (define legal rights, duties, privileges and functions)	**To persuade**
create, *e.g.* deeds, contracts, leases, wills and trusts through modifying precedents	create court documents, *e.g.* pleadings and affidavits

Figure 2-4

form of advocacy. Because these documents come under close scrutiny by courts and adversaries and because lawyers must adhere to certain formalities in preparing them most lawyers say that they draft, rather than write, them.

4. Negotiation

What a client wants almost always conflicts with what other people want. This lies at the heart of most clients' legal problems. The interview helps to get the problem-solving process started but negotiation occurs further down the line. If interviewing is listening, questioning and advising, negotiation is listening, questioning and resolving conflicts. Interviewing is the skill of interacting with clients to help them solve problems; negotiation is the skill of interacting with others to resolve conflict.

In a playing-out conflict problem, in which the client's goal may be to win as much as possible while risking as little as possible, lawyers often use the threat of litigation or continued litigation together with negotiation as part of an overall strategy to achieve that goal. The lawyer may ultimately achieve a successful settlement in that the client gets something, the litigation is terminated, and the client avoids the risk of trial.[12]

In a conflict-blocking problem, the client's goal may be to enter into, or complete, an agreement from which he or she hopes to benefit. One of the lawyer's functions is to negotiate and draft the agreement so that the client gets as many advantages as possible, and all potential conflicts are blocked. To achieve this lawyers use standard documents or precedents which are modified to reflect negotiation outcomes, and bargaining power. For example, lawyers for sellers know that sellers would like more security for payment than buyers are prepared to give. On the other side, lawyers for buyers know that buyers would like more warranties than sellers are prepared to give. If the buyers have greater bargaining power, their lawyers are likely to negotiate the provision of less security and more warranties — and vice versa if the sellers have greater bargaining power.[13]

5. Advocacy

When negotiation breaks down in a playing-out conflict situation, lawyers rely on advocacy. Advocacy is the skill of persuasion. Because it is dependent on such a variety of skills, attitudes and knowledge, it is probably the most complex and challenging of all legal skills. It is dependent on component skills such as listening, questioning, research, analysis, synthesis and planning. It is also dependent on the other core legal skills such as interviewing, writing and drafting. Skilful advocacy is especially dependent on professional attitudes such as dedication, professionalism and self-control, as well as on sound substantive and procedural legal knowledge and non-legal, worldly knowledge.

Because advocacy is so complex, its most important component skill may well be synthesis, or the ability to bring things together. How do advocates bring all their skills and knowledge together in harmony to make them work for the client? From the first interview to the appearance in court, they try to develop a complete theory of the case.

> "A complete theory of the case combines legal theories and descriptive and explanatory hypotheses in a story which has both rational and psychological appeal. It is a theory that describes what happened and why in a way that is persuasive both to the mind and to the heart."[14]

In short, a theory of the case is a story designed to persuade logically and emotionally.

The best advocates work on a case from two perspectives. On one hand, they focus on developing this theory. On the other hand, they sort through a great mass of factual detail. To reconcile these two perspectives, they bring theory and facts closer together in two ways: they look for patterns in the mass of facts to formulate a theory that will strengthen their case; having developed a theory they then look for factual details to support it. In advocacy, the client's goal is to win; the lawyer's goal is to find and arrange details to fit the theory, and then to reformulate the theory so that it fits the details.[15]

3. Knowledge

Knowledge, the last of the three requirements of competent lawyering, falls into two basic classifications: non-legal and legal knowledge.

Non-legal knowledge

If you are going to be a construction lawyer, it is necessary to have some non-legal knowledge about construction engineering. If you are going to be the managing partner of a law firm or head of the litigation department, you should know about management. If you do commercial litigation and are in the habit of cross-examining accountants, you should be knowledgeable about accounting, and if you are doing planning law, you should be familiar with environmental problems.

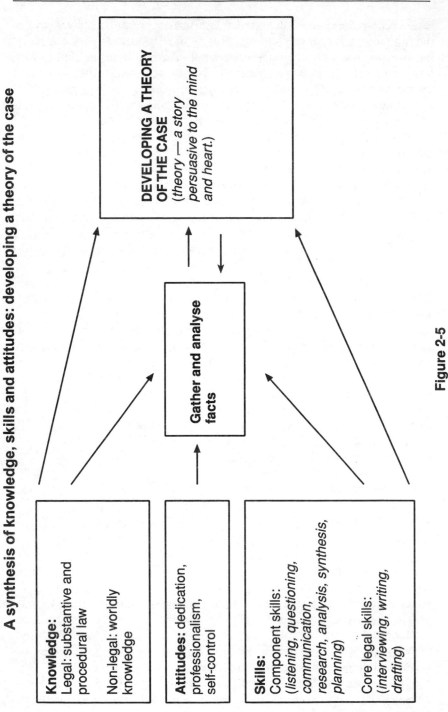

A synthesis of knowledge, skills and attitudes: developing a theory of the case

DEVELOPING A THEORY OF THE CASE
(*theory — a story persuasive to the mind and heart.*)

Gather and analyse facts

Knowledge:
Legal: substantive and procedural law

Non-legal: worldly knowledge

Attitudes: dedication, professionalism, self-control

Skills:
Component skills:
(*listening, questioning, communication, research, analysis, synthesis, planning*)

Core legal skills:
(*interviewing, writing, drafting*)

Figure 2-5

There is no point practising personal injury law, if you do not understand the fundamentals of medical practice or medical terminology. Determining what non-legal knowledge is necessary for law practice depends in large measure on what area of practice you are aiming for and where your interests lie.

Just as important as having specific areas of non-legal knowledge at your disposal, however, is to regard the whole of your background, training and experience as a foundation and a resource for practising law. It stands to reason that the broader the life experience of the lawyer the more resources the lawyer brings to the job. Lawyers who have a limited life experience or a narrow viewpoint can easily do a disservice to their clients. Not knowing fundamental truths about people, lawyers, judges, history or society can create blind spots that undermine the lawyer's problem-solving strategies.

One of the most famous examples of this phenomenon occurred in the criminal trial involving *Lady Chatterley's Lover*, a trial in which Penguin Books, publisher of one of D.H. Lawrence's best known novels, was tried under the obscenity laws. The jury had to decide if the book was obscene beyond a reasonable doubt: did it tend to deprave and corrupt the minds of those who read it? The trial took place in 1962, a time of change in Britain when people were finally overcoming the privations of the post-war era, and the middle classes were becoming more numerous and prosperous. Barriers of class and privilege were crumbling, and ordinary people were getting used to the idea that they, too, had a right to satisfy material, intellectual and emotional needs that went beyond mere survival.

In *Lady Chatterley's Lover*, a love story involving a gamekeeper and an upper-class woman, the democratisation of needs-satisfaction was a main theme: everybody, including gamekeepers and upper-class women, were entitled to enjoy life, in particular to enjoy sex. Although the story took place between the wars, this needs-satisfaction theme mirrored what many people were concerned about in the early 1960s. This aspect, however, appears to have been lost on the prosecution. Not only did it misunderstand the social environment in which it was operating, it failed to appreciate that the jury was part of that environment. In the Crown's opening address to the jury, Mr Griffith-Jones, Senior Treasury Counsel at the Old Bailey, raised a moral issue with the following:

"You may think that one of the ways in which you can test this book, and test it from the most liberal outlook, is to ask yourselves the question, when you have read it through, would you approve of your young sons, young daughters — because girls can read as well as boys

— reading this book? Is it a book you would have lying around your own house?"[16]

But then he pushed his own moral argument off the rails, revealing a social blind spot that must have left the jury frowning. He said: "Is it a book that you would even wish your wife or your servants to read?"[17]

This delightful anecdote, well-known in legal circles, underscores the importance for lawyers of understanding the world in which they live.

Legal knowledge

The second category of knowledge is legal knowledge. Lawyers need to be familiar with two main areas of legal knowledge: substantive and procedural law and transactional information.

Substantive and procedural law

Substantive and procedural law are combined here because they are both subjects concerned with legal rules. Charles Rembar distinguishes substantive law from procedural law this way:

> "Substantive law consists of rights we are said to have and duties we are told we must accept. Procedural law is the set of instructions prescribing how we redress a violated right, how our neglected duties are imposed. In the absence of a will, widow and children take the land: this is a rule of substantive law. The defendant has 20 days in which to answer plaintiff's complaint: this is a rule of procedure."[18]

Substantive law is what lawyers need to know in order to advise their clients of their rights and obligations. In a playing-out conflict situation, if you do not know the substantive law, it is impossible to advise clients what they are entitled to get, or obligated to do. In a conflict-blocking situation, it is difficult to design documents and legal transactions to anticipate substantive legal issues and block conflicts if you do not know substantive law.

Procedural law is a set of rules that establishes pathways for getting what your client is entitled to. It also sets up obstacles to what other people may want from your client. For example, if you do not follow correct procedures within prescribed times, or you do not know how to implement these procedures, you may undermine your client's substantive rights. Conversely, if an opposite party makes procedural errors, you need to know how to take advantage of them in order to strengthen your client's substantive rights or alleviate the burden of your client's obligations.

The above examples and the emphasis law schools place on substantive and procedural law should be sufficient to convince everyone that lawyers need to be well-educated in law. But a school of thought has evolved that seems to downgrade legal knowledge in favour of legal skills.

The idea that lawyers can be skilful without knowing the law has been around for a long time. Peter Birks has explained how even the ancient Romans debated the knowledge-versus-skills controversy. Referring to a debate in Cicero's *De Oratore*, Birks says that one side claims that all an advocate needs is "native wit and personal skills," while the other side, in the person of Crassus, says that "nothing is more disgraceful than to hold yourself out to defend a client's interests, only to wreck his hopes because the study of law has been beneath your notice."[19]

"Quod tamen os est illius patroni, qui ad eas causas sine ulla scientia iuris audet accedere (What a nerve a barrister has who dares to involve himself in such cases without any learning in the law)!"[20]

Today, supporters of the "skills-over-knowledge" school continue to suggest knowing the law should take a back seat to being proficient in skills. They favour legal skills over legal knowledge on the ground that legal skills are transferable — they can be used in a wide variety of legal transactions. Good advocates, goes the argument, can transfer their skills to any type of legal problem and still be effective, whereas knowledge of the law is much more transaction-specific. Besides, skills take years to acquire and are not easily lost, but knowledge of the law can fade in one's memory and, in any event, the law is always changing.

Some proponents of the skills-over-knowledge school take the argument further. They say that lawyers do not necessarily need their heads filled with legal knowledge, they just have to know how to find it. They must be able to learn what they need to know in pertinent areas of practice. Thus, it is more important to have the "skill of acquiring knowledge," such as skill in legal research, than to be able instantly to recall legal knowledge.

Many practising lawyers do not subscribe to this theory. According to one study of lawyer competence, the most important characteristic identified by lawyers as necessary for competence is "knowledge of substantive law".[21] In a similar study, knowledge of substantive law ranked, in importance, ahead of the skills of legal research, negotiation and drafting, although below such skills as fact-gathering, and effective oral expression.[22]

To many lawyers, it is indisputable that recall and understanding of legal knowledge are essential to competence. An advocate in the middle of a trial does not have time to do legal research. He or she has to know the law of evidence in order to make objections and, if necessary, to support them with legal argument. A lawyer interviewing a client about an accident she has suffered must know about the law of damages to guide the questioning process. A lawyer studying a commercial agreement for a client has to know the applicable law in order to interpret the agreement sensibly. A lawyer in the midst of transferring real estate for a vendor client who suddenly wants to back out of the deal has to know the law of contract in order to advise the client. A criminal lawyer trying to mitigate sentence for a client who has just been convicted, must know the law of sentencing. A lawyer who is called to the hospital to draft a will for a dying client must know the key provisions of wills law and procedure; not knowing an important rule could result in an invalid will and angry beneficiaries who sue because they did not obtain what they were supposed to under the will.

In all these situations, lawyers cannot rely solely on research skills to do a good job. They either must respond immediately with the appropriate knowledge or have sufficient depth of understanding to complete the job with minimal top-up research. Lawyers who have a great deal of legal knowledge stored in their memory that can be quickly recalled are undoubtedly more competent because they know automatically what the client's options are. The simplest answer to the knowledge/skills controversy is that both are important. People learning how to be lawyers should treat knowledge and skills with equal respect and people teaching others how to be lawyers need to balance the two.

Students may find the legal knowledge that lawyers need has more layers and greater depth than they are used to. Legal knowledge is not just knowing the laws and how they apply to specific situations. Nor is it enough to be able, with that knowledge, to identify legal issues and construct legal arguments. Competent lawyers need to understand law in contexts that extend beyond the narrow application of rules.

When lawyers are negotiating, advising or advocating, they make statements about rights and obligations. It is beneficial for clients that behind those statements the lawyer has a depth of understanding based on the moral, psychological, economic, historical or other implications of the situation and the relevant law. Good lawyers need to be able to interpret the law in this wider context. They need to understand the principles and purposes behind it. The following example helps to illustrate why this understanding is necessary.

Substantive-law problem

Alice had just purchased an expensive stereo from a hi-fi dealer. On the day the dealer installed it, she gave him a cheque for the full purchase price. The next day the stereo stopped functioning. She telephoned the dealer who said he would send someone to her house in two days to see what he could do. Alice, worried that she had been sold a defective stereo, telephoned a young friend of hers, Foster, who had recently become a lawyer. Obviously upset, she asked him if she could stop payment on the cheque.

"Sure you can," Foster said, after listening patiently to her story. "But unless you can prove that the dealer defrauded you or that the stereo is absolutely worthless, he can rightfully demand you make good that cheque. And if you don't, he can sue you and win. Just because the stereo is not working, it doesn't mean it's worthless or that he has defrauded you."

"But I don't want to pay for it until I know the stereo is functional. Isn't that reasonable?"

"The problem is," said Foster, "you have already paid for it. The courts look at cheques as if they are practically cash. Once you write that cheque, it's like an unconditional promise to pay. You can't back out of it just because you're not completely satisfied. The law regards cheques in this way, because if it didn't, people would be writing cheques and stopping payment at the drop of a hat. That wouldn't be very good for commerce. It would make commercial transactions very risky for the merchant."

"I can see your point," said Alice thoughtfully, but then she turned irate. "But I can still go to the bank and put a stop on that cheque, can't I? And if I do, I'm sure that guy will be a lot quicker about replacing my stereo than going to see his lawyer to sue me. What do you think?"

"Maybe so, Alice. The decision, of course, is yours. But let me get a little more information from you first..."

Alice and Foster discussed this situation several times and Alice eventually decided not to stop payment on the cheque but, instead, to work things out with the dealer. She really wanted a good stereo system and Foster had reminded her that the dealer would be the one servicing the stereo guarantee for the next year. It might be a good idea, he advised, to start the relationship off on a friendly basis rather than on a confrontational one.

Foster's advice turned out to be helpful to Alice. She particularly liked the way he clarified the law of cheques in relation to its commercial purpose. It added a moral dimension to her decision-making, so that making a legal decision also meant doing the right thing. She also thought his reminder about the importance of starting off on the right foot with the dealer was timely; it calmed her anger because it helped her see how unlikely it was that the dealer deliberately cheated her. Foster's knowledge of law and commerce, as well as psychology, gave his advice considerable depth.

Understanding principles and purposes is particularly important to lawyers in procedural law, because procedural rules are often complicated and difficult to explain to clients. Consider this example.

Procedural-law problem

A client, Phil, who was owed money had a strong case against the debtor, David, against whom he had brought legal action. Phil's lawyer, Susanna, brought on an application for summary judgment which calls for a judge's decision based on evidence in affidavits filed by the client and the debtor. David, in his affidavit, put forward a defence which, in Phil's view, was a complete lie. Susanna's view, however, was that the lie could not be disproved unless there were a full trial with witnesses and cross-examination. She explained to Phil that it was very unlikely she would win the summary–judgment application, because all David had to show was that he had an arguable case, after which the judge would refer the matter to the trial court. The case would therefore not be resolved for at least another year. A sophisticated client, Phil wanted an explanation from his lawyer: how could the law allow David to frustrate his claim for another year?

Susanna sympathised with her client's frustration and could see he needed an explanation. "Plaintiffs do not like long drawn-out cases, but that is the nature of litigation, I'm sorry to say. In order to protect the rights of the parties and ensure that each side's case is fully aired, procedures can be lengthy."

"But he's lying," said Phil, "and he's using the legal system to delay, while he holds on to my money."

"That may be true," said Susanna, "but look at it this way: the summary–judgment procedure is an effort by the law to try to remedy some of the inconvenience of protracted litigation. In order to get judgment summarily, in other words, to deprive your opponent of his day in court, your case has to be so overwhelming and his so weak that the court has to be able to say, on looking at the documentary evidence alone, the defendant doesn't stand a chance. It's one way the law tries to balance the principle of individual rights against the need for efficiency in the legal system. That's the purpose of this procedure."

When Susanna got into court to argue that her client should get summary judgment, she reminded the judge of that purpose, and argued further that the strict rules of summary judgment should not be used by people to delay justice. She asked the judge to look carefully at David's affidavit, pointed out some inconsistencies in it, and urged the judge to find that it was quite possible he was not telling the truth.

"You can prevent the defendant from using the court to delay justice while he keeps my client's money, yet still preserve his right to be heard by ordering him to pay the amount owed into court pending the outcome of trial," she concluded. The judge agreed and he so ordered.

Susanna's understanding of the law went beyond the ability to argue that the case fell within certain rules related to summary judgment. According to the rules she had a weak case for summary judgment. But her understanding of the purpose of summary-judgment law and the competing principles it tries to reconcile helped her put her client's case before the court in a way that appealed logically and emotionally to the judge. Because of Susanna's argument, he made an order that applied the law in a way that fulfilled its original purpose.

Transactional information

Substantive and procedural law is a great part of the legal knowledge that lawyers need. One final component, however, is necessary to round out that knowledge. It is a catchall category called *transactional information*.

Transactional information needs to be explained by reference to the concept of *transaction*, sometimes referred to as a "legal task."[23] A transaction is defined as a job done by a lawyer characterised by steps or procedures[24] and governed by legal rules and practices specific to that transaction. Types of transactions include *civil litigation, criminal litigation, real-property conveyance, corporate acquisition*, a *will*, creation of a *trust* and *public company flotation*. Transactions have sub-types. *Civil litigation* can have *divorce* as a sub-type. *Real-property conveyance* can have *residential conveyance* as a sub-type.

Transactions involve either playing-out or blocking problems. A personal injury action is a playing-out conflict transaction; it begins when the client comes into the office with a problem and it ends when a legal action is tried or settled. A corporate acquisition is a conflict-blocking transaction which begins with a buyer who has reached a preliminary agreement to buy a business and ends at completion when documents are signed and money changes hands. Transactional information is the legal information a lawyer needs to move successfully from the beginning to the end of the transaction. This is usually information about standard documents and procedures to use for specific transactions, as well as local practices for expediting them. In a real-property conveyance, examples of transactional information would include where to do the title search for a specific property, which standard forms to use in a specific situation and procedures for dealing with the estate agent's commission or with banks lending money to purchasers.

PUTTING TOGETHER KNOWLEDGE, SKILLS AND ATTITUDES

How does the lawyer put knowledge, skills and attitudes together to solve a client's problem and successfully complete a transaction? To answer this question and conclude this chapter, let us take a brief look at a divorce. A divorce is a type of legal transaction designed to meet a variety of client and social goals. The client may want to alleviate her or his misery, and to divide property and income; society wants to assign responsibility for dependants. Lawyers need to know the substantive and procedural law related to these issues — grounds for divorce, property-division laws, child-maintenance and custody laws as well as how to get into court to raise these issues and prove the client's entitlements.

The lawyer needs skills such as interviewing, negotiating and advocating to perform the transaction. The lawyer will probably need drafting skills to draft the settlement agreement that the parties reach in many cases. The lawyer also needs a variety of basic transactional information such as where, when and how to file the divorce petition, and what other documents to file. In addition, the lawyer needs to know more complex transactional information such as knowing the strategies for stopping spouses from disposing of assets or kidnapping children, and knowing which psychiatrists write the most sympathetic reports.

The lawyer also needs to exhibit conduct that reflects a variety of attitudes. The lawyer needs to adopt a professional stance so that the client receives objective advice. Yet the lawyer needs to be sympathetic to the client's suffering. The lawyer must behave ethically and, where children are involved, adhere to special rules that sometimes place their interests above those of the client. The lawyer needs to be wily and tough because in divorce litigation, husbands and wives can see themselves as enemies in a battle for survival, resorting to the most aggressive manoeuvres to win. The lawyer needs to be flexible and realise when the parties are ready to quit fighting and talk settlement.

[1] Kim Economides and Jeff Smallcombe, *Preparatory Skills Training for Trainee Solicitors* (Law Society of England and Wales, London, 1991).

[2] American Bar Association, *Legal Education and Professional Development — An Educational Continuum* (Report on the Task Force on Law Schools and the Profession: Narrowing the Gap) (MacCrate Report, 1992).

[3] *The National*, Vol. 18, No. 8, October 1991, p.2.

[4] See excerpt from "Attitudes of a Profession" (1957) 2 *Social Work* 4, in *Lawyers*, eds Julian Disney, Paul Redmond, John Basten and Stan Ross (The Law Book Company. NSW, 2nd ed., 1968), p.74.

[5] Code of Conduct of the Bar of England and Wales (Adopted by the Bar Council, January 27, 1990), Part II, Fundamental Principles 203(a).

[6] John L. Jenkins, *The Litigators* (Doubleday, New York, 1989), pp.238–239.

[7] See excerpt from "Misleading on Identity in Court" (1981) 7 *Commonwealth Law Bulletin* 285, in *Lawyers*, eds Julian Disney, Paul Redmond, John Basten and Stan Ross (The Law Book Company, NSW, 2nd ed., 1968), p.899.

[8] Allan Williams, Paul Dobson, Mike Walters, *Changing Culture: New Organisational Approaches* (Institute of Personnel Management, London, 1989), p.42.

[9] David A. Binder and Susan C. Price, *Legal Interviewing and Counselling—A Client–Centered Approach* (West Publishing Co., St Paul, Minn., 1977), p.1.

[10] Robert Dick Q.C., *Legal Drafting* (The Carswell Company, Toronto, 2nd ed., 1985), p.1.

[11] Drafting and conflict-blocking will be dealt with in more detail in Chaps. 7 and 8.

[12] Playing-out conflict negotiation is discussed further in Chap. 6.

[13] Blocking-conflict negotiation is discussed further in Chap. 8.

[14] David A. Binder and Paul Bergman, *Fact Investigation: From Hypothesis To Proof* (West Publishing, St Paul, Minn. 1984), p.184.

[15] Aspects of advocacy are discussed further in Chap. 6.

[16] C.H. Rolph (ed)., *The Trial of Lady Chatterley—Regina v. Penguin Books Limited* (Penguin Books, Middlesex, 1961), p.17.

[17] *ibid.*

[18] Charles Rembar, *The Law of the Land* (Simon & Schuster, New York, 1980), p.77.

[19] See Peter Birks, "Adjudication and Interpretation in the Common Law" (1994) 1 *Legal Studies* 156–170 at 157.

[20] *ibid.*

[21] John De Groot, "Acquiring Basic Legal Skills and Knowledge", (1994) 12 *Journal of Professional Legal Education* 1–16 at 2.

[22] F.K. Zemans and V.G. Rosenblum, *The Making of a Public Profession* (Chicago, American Bar Foundation, 1981), cited in John De Groot, *ibid.*, pp.2–3.

[23] Christopher Roper, "The Legal Practice Courses—Theoretical Frameworks and Models" (1988) 6 *Journal of Professional Legal Education* 77–86 at 78.

[24] Stephen Nathanson, "Putting Skills and Transactions Together in Professional Legal Training" (1987) 5 *Journal of Profession Legal Education* 187–200 at 187.

CHAPTER 3

THE PROCESS OF LEGAL PROBLEM SOLVING

PROBLEM-SOLVING AT THE CENTRE OF WHAT LAWYERS DO[1]

From an educational perspective, competence may be the aggregate of knowledge, skills and attitudes, but competence in action is the ability to solve legal problems. Whether lawyers are handling a playing-out or blocking situation, problem solving is at the centre of what they do. Law students need to be aware of this and try to make learning to solve legal problems their primary educational goal. They should plan their education so that they learn the knowledge, skills and attitudes necessary to solving a wide variety of legal problems. The following diagram illustrates how knowledge, skills and attitudes are related to legal problem-solving and competence.

Competence in legal practice

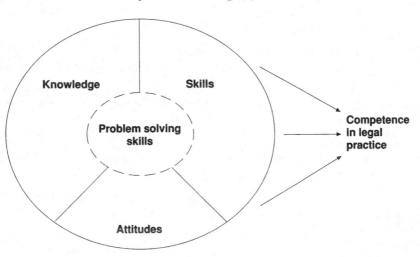

Figure 3-1

Since problem-solving skill is the essence of competent legal practice, it would be helpful to have a model or framework for solving legal problems — a *process model* illustrating both a general theory of legal practice and the process of solving legal problems. Process models are useful because they reinforce the idea that people should solve complicated problems by going through a process. They can begin at the beginning, and proceed through stages. Another rationale for using a process model is that in tense situations when clear thinking should prevail, one can follow a premeditated series of steps to solve problems.

Process models have been used in other professions (such as management and medicine) for many years.[2] They have also been used in legal education,[3] but very sparingly, since they have not yet gained wide acceptance as either practical or theoretical tools. The model described in this chapter is both practical — lawyers can use it to help them deal with real-life problems — and theoretical, because it presents a general, though simplified, theory of legal practice.

Following a logical sequence of stages, the model offers a systematic way of tackling a wide range of legal problems. This does not mean one can, or should, follow the model rigidly with every problem; legal problems are too different from one another to attempt that. Nonetheless, lawyers can follow a similar process to tackle most legal problems. The model allows for flexibility in order to accommodate the variety and complexity of legal problems lawyers need to solve.

Stage one of the process is *problem and goal definition*. Stage two is *fact investigation*. Stage three is *legal issue identification and assessment*. Stage four is *advice and decision making*. Stage five is *planning and implementation*.

The model identifies all legal problems as client goals in conflict with various obstacles. These obstacles may be created by law or by the goals of other parties, including lawyers confronted with their own goals, or the profession's ethical constraints. Problems are satisfactorily solved when client goals are met by overcoming the obstacles, or otherwise reconciling goals, in ways that are acceptable to clients.

Conflict is, without doubt, the main theme in legal problem solving. Lawyers are constantly trying to foresee and block it, and when it occurs, to play it out by winning or resolving it. In the various stages of the problem-solving process, lawyers must pay attention not only to the goals of the client, but also try to understand what the other parties' goals are, since these will normally conflict with the client's. It is important to define the whole problem, from the first stage onwards, in a way that takes into account the goals of everyone involved, including adversaries, courts, regulatory authorities, government departments and other lawyers.

Problem and goal definition is discussed below as the first of five stages.

A process model of legal problem solving

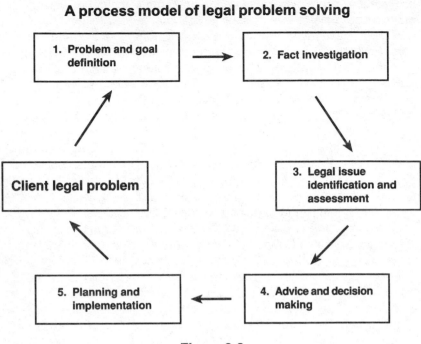

Figure 3-2

THE STAGES OF LEGAL PROBLEM SOLVING

1. Problem and goal definition

In this first stage, the problem itself is defined. The client's, as well as other parties', goals are identified. What does the client want or need? What are the obstacles? How can they be overcome?

The nature of a problem may change over time, as goals and attitudes change, or new problems may arise as facts are gathered, and steps are taken to solve it. The problem may have to undergo redefinition. Problem and goal definition is not a stagnant stage.

To use a simple example, a client charged with a criminal offence may expect his lawyer to obtain an acquittal, but as information is gathered from the prosecution before trial it may appear that the evidence against the client is overwhelming. Lawyer and client begin to evaluate the benefits of a guilty plea. The client's goal changes from wanting an acquittal, to attracting the lightest sentence possible.

Although the definition of what the problem really is may be revised many times, a diagnosis must be made at the beginning in order to give the problem-solving process momentum and direction. The most important feature of this first stage is to define the client's goals — even in the most general way — and those of the other parties. If this is not done, the lawyer may not be able to proceed effectively.

2. Fact Investigation

In this stage, the lawyer gathers facts through interviews, correspondence, document analysis and other means in order to identify legal issues and assess them in relation to the problem. Fact investigation theoretically precedes legal-issue identification, although in real life one cannot pursue all the facts without having a preliminary idea of the legal issues, which gives direction to the investigation. Even so, fact investigation precedes legal-issue identification in this model, mainly because in real life the lawyer has to get *some* facts first before identifying legal issues.

In this stage, as well as in the first one, a variety of different skills are useful. The lawyer must be able to build rapport with the client, frame effective questions and organise the investigation so that information is accurately and efficiently collected. The lawyer must also have a sound knowledge of the legal issues because it is these that move the fact-investigation process forward. The following anecdote, recounted by a young lawyer, illustrates the importance of being conversant with relevant legal issues in the fact-investigation stage.

> I once saw a client in a typical slip-and-fall case. She slipped and fell outside a shop and suffered severe back injuries. I began to question her, looking for evidence of negligence. What substance was on the surface of the walkway? What was she doing at the time? Were there any warning signs? And so forth. I noted the date the mishap occurred. I knew that if the client wanted to sue, she had to do so within three years of the mishap or be barred from suit. I also could tell that the mishap had probably occurred on municipal property. But what I did *not* know was that if someone wanted to sue the municipality, a notice of the claim had to be sent by letter to the municipality within 90 days of the accident. Not knowing this simple legal point, I failed immediately to investigate who owned the property on which the slippery surface was found (it later turned out to be the municipality) and I did not ask whether the client had written to the municipality to notify them of the accident. (Luckily for me, she had written them a complaint letter.)
>
> After I discovered my error, I changed the firm's personal-injury

information forms. Now, after clients fill in the form, and lawyers review it, there are two tick boxes for them to check:

Possibility of municipal responsibility ☐

If yes, notification sent? ☐

3. Legal-issue identification and assessment

Although a preliminary identification of issues is needed in Stage 2 to give direction to fact investigation, legal-issue identification and assessment is really a separate stage. It has its own distinct purposes which are to identify legal issues raised by the facts, and to assess these issues in relation to decisions that need to be made.

Law students are familiar with identifying legal issues; they look at facts and identify which legal issues are relevant to deciding the case. When legal issues are *assessed*, a prediction is made as to which side would win should the issues be litigated, or whether or not someone can maintain a credible position on either side of an issue.

(a) Prediction assessment

Weighing the legal merits of both sides of an issue and predicting which side would win if the issue goes to court is called a *prediction assessment*. In law school, students are often taught that a well-argued *prediction assessment* is *the* solution to the problem. But in real-life legal problem-solving, where the problem involves the client's personal decisions about what steps to take, *prediction assessment* is only one of several factors to take into account. To illustrate the point, in a playing-out conflict situation, a lawyer may research a case and say to a client: "I think you will win because the facts of your case fall within the law." Then, to help the client, the lawyer moves into Stage 4 of problem-solving — *advice and decision-making*. In that stage, the lawyer examines other factors in addition to predicting the probability of winning in order to help the client make a decision.

Prediction assessments are useful in the process of decision-making, particularly in dealing with playing-out conflict decisions such as whether to sue, negotiate, settle a conflict on certain terms and what strategy to adopt in litigation. But other factors such as peace of mind and cost in time or money need also to be considered.

(b) Credible-position assessment

Used mostly in conflict-blocking decisions, the other type of legal-issue assessment is *credible-position assessment*. In credible-position assessment, the lawyer tries to answer this question: given a specific legal issue, can my client's opponent maintain a credible position arguing for the other side. For example, suppose your client, Ms Stuart, has instructed you to arrange the purchase of a house from the seller, Mr Cooper. A search of the land registry reveals Mr Cooper is the sole owner. Ms Stuart tells you in passing that she thought Mr Cooper was not married, but when she viewed the house she noticed that a woman, Ms Logan, was living there with him. You identify a legal issue: it is possible that Ms Logan has a non-registered, equitable interest in the house by virtue of her relationship with Mr Cooper. It is also possible that Ms Stuart has constructive notice of that interest. This means that even after the house is conveyed from Mr Cooper to Ms Stuart, Ms Logan could still claim an interest in the house and enforce her right by suing Ms Stuart.

Of course, the likelihood of this occurring is small. But in the unlikely event this scenario were to unfold, the key question is, would Ms Logan's lawyer be able to maintain a credible position? In other words, would that lawyer have a credible, even if somewhat flimsy, legal argument in her favour? If so, then on Ms Stuart's behalf, you could consider making a decision to reduce the risk by blocking the potential conflict. Legal conflict is costly even if your client is likely to win. You can block the conflict for your client by asking if Ms Logan would be prepared to sign a release or a confirmation that she has no interest in the house. If she refuses, Ms Stuart can consider backing out of the deal. If she agrees then the potential conflict can be blocked.

4. Advice and decision-making

Once the goals, facts and issues are thoroughly explored, the lawyer can go on to *advice and decision-making*. It is useful to view the advice and decision-making stage in three sub-stages: *developing options, evaluating options* and, *choosing the best option*.

(a) Developing options

Developing options is probably the most intellectually challenging of the three sub-stages. Here, an ability to see the relationships between different aspects and stages of the problem is essential. The lawyer has to consider the goals, facts and issues, then identify the options available to solve the client's problem. Lawyers can consider many options, examples being to negotiate, mediate, litigate, hire an expert, draft a particular document, write a letter or go to trial. Lawyers can do various other things or combinations of them or devise something completely new and original.

They also consider options that are tried and true or what are called *standard solutions* to problems. Much of the lawyer's store of transactional information is filled with standard solutions that were developed by others to solve particular problems.

In the playing-out conflict arena, a good example often cited is the "structured settlement" in personal injury cases.[4] Instead of negotiating a lump-sum payment from an insurer to compensate a severely injured plaintiff, lawyers can sometimes negotiate a periodic payment designed principally to rehabilitate plaintiffs. This can meet the goals of both the plaintiff — who wants to avoid the risk of managing a large amount of money but needs to receive a guarantee of ongoing care for life — and the goals of the insurer — who wants to avoid the expense of a large lump-sum payment by paying an annuity for life.

In the conflict-blocking arena, a simple example of this sort is to use a third-party expert to decide something. In the sale of a group of assets the parties cannot always agree on the value of one or more assets, but they still want to complete the sale. So they agree to hire an expert on valuation whose opinion is final and binding. They draft a provision to close off the possibility that the expert's opinion will ever be reviewed by a court, because they want to avoid or block a costly legal conflict.

These are solutions to problems that may once have challenged lawyers' creative problem-solving ability, but are now just standard solutions developed and refined over time. When no standard solution fits, however, the lawyer needs to use his or her creative problem-solving ability to invent something new. To develop options effectively, lawyers need to be both creative as well as able to recall a wide variety of standard solutions.

(b) Evaluating options

In this second stage of advice and decision-making, lawyers evaluate the risks and benefits of each option. Consider this example of a playing-out conflict problem: a lawyer handling a lawsuit has been offered £25,000 to settle a legal action. The lawyer's fees and expenses would amount to £5000. This would put £20,000 in the client's hands. The lawyer has already done a prediction assessment and has given the client an estimate of the chances of success at trial:

"You've got about a 50% chance of success if you go to trial. If you win you could get about £50,000 after deducting legal fees. Let's look at your options. Option 1: the settlement option is worth about £20,000. Option 2: the trial option is worth about £25,000 (50% × £50,000)."

If the probability factor is accurate, and looked at in purely financial terms, the trial option is the most beneficial choice. The strategy for reaching this decision is called an *optimising* strategy. It quantifies options and identifies the one with the highest payoff.[5] But an optimising strategy that focuses only on probabilities and financial outcomes is usually too rigid for clients. Although probabilities are useful for giving guidance to clients, it is nonetheless difficult to predict outcomes in court — many events can change the course of a trial. Things can happen in a courtroom that lawyers cannot predict. This unpredictability does not mean calculating probabilities is useless, but it does mean things can occur that the clients feel they never bargained for. Decision-making should depend not only on an analysis of financial outcomes but also on non-financial outcomes, such as the unpredictability of trials, the client's appetite for risk, the stress that might be caused or the precious time involved in going to trial.[6]

One challenge new lawyers have with this stage is that they find it difficult to evaluate options when they do not know what the possible consequences are really like. How would they know what could possibly happen at a trial — especially the emotional highs and lows of unpredictable events — unless they have experienced one themselves? In a conflict-blocking situation, how would they know the consequences of not conducting an expensive investigation into the value of an asset their client wants to purchase when they have not experienced the satisfaction derived from a successful investigation or the panic of discovering serious errors because of not doing an investigation? To learn about consequences, new lawyers must consult more senior lawyers who have had the necessary first-hand experience. That is why one of the most important strategies for evaluating options is to consult senior lawyers.

(c) Choosing the best option

In choosing options, two kinds of decision-making are used. In the first, the lawyer presents the client with options along with their consequences, but the client makes the ultimate decision. Binder and Price, authors of a classic textbook on legal interviewing, call this client-centred decision-making.[7] In the second kind, the lawyer recommends, or actually makes, the decision, after evaluating options with or without consulting the client. This is lawyer-centred decision-making.

Client-centred decision-making comes out of a participatory philosophy of problem-solving.[8] Since it is the client who has to live with the decision, the lawyer should fully disclose risks and benefits of various options. This process of disclosure and the client's participation in the decision minimises grounds for subsequent client grievance and increases client satisfaction by helping the client achieve a measure of control over his or her life.[9]

But clients should not make all the decisions and many situations exist in which client participation in the decision-making process should be limited. James Freund differentiates decisions according to the scope of their significance to the client. He says that big decisions should be client-centred, and small ones, lawyer-centred. The big decision, which he calls "go/no-go", is a choice between action and inaction on some significant matter, such as whether to start a lawsuit or a corporate acquisition. The small decision, which is called "way-to-go", involves less important choices and operates on the premise that the client has already decided to do something and the question is what options are available to carry it out.[10]

One difficulty, especially for new lawyers, is to be able to identify which decisions should be client-centred and which lawyer-centred. Sometimes the answer is easy because it is set out clearly in ethical rules. For example, decisions about whether or not to commence or defend civil proceedings, testify as a defendant or plead guilty in a criminal proceeding all require the client's consent, preferably in writing.[11] These rules make sense because the decisions are obviously important to the client in any situation.

In most situations, however, the rules are not clear and much depends on the relationship between lawyer and client. Some clients want to play a part in every decision no matter how minor and others give the lawyer wide discretion to make decisions. It is always best to clarify with the client at the beginning what kind of relationship is the most workable and to establish clear, written guidelines for decision-making.

5. Planning and implementation

Some planning may already have taken place in the early part of Stage 4, during options-development, because options have to be developed and plans outlined before client and lawyer can evaluate them. But later, in the planning and implementation stage, the decision is more fully developed and carried out. The plan may be as comprehensive as an entire transaction: for example, lawyer and client may decide after evaluating options to begin litigation or to set up a trust. Or the plan may be very simple — to write a letter or arrange a negotiation meeting.

Planning and implementation—developing a plan

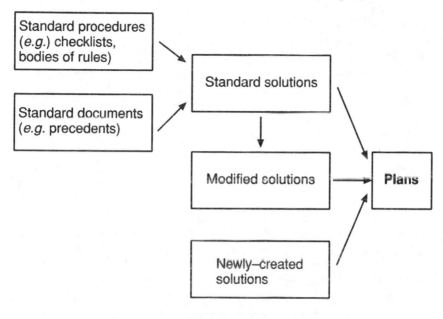

Figure 3-3

The plans should indicate sequence and timing of actions, and who does what. They can be based on *standard solutions* or be *newly created*. Standard solutions consist of *standard procedures*, sometimes found in checklists or bodies of rules,[12] and *standard documents* often referred to as *precedents*.

When the transaction is simple, standard solutions can sometimes be followed with little difficulty. In most cases, however, they must be modified because no two problems are the same. An example is the use of precedent court forms, which need to be modified in most cases. Since court forms are usually an instrument of persuasion, modification does not mean just filling in blanks, but thoughtful and creative adaptation in order to persuade. When lawyers develop modifications, the results are called *modified solutions*. A simple example of a modified solution is the personal-injury information form, changed by the lawyer who realized the municipality had to be notified with 90 days if legal action was contemplated against it, (see pages 41–42).

For some legal transactions, standard solutions may be unavailable or of little value. In these cases, lawyers need to develop *newly-created solutions*. Figure 3-3 following diagram gives an idea of the relationship between the various planning concepts just introduced.

LINEARITY AND FLEXIBILITY

For the legal problem-solver, one important feature worth paying attention to, particularly in the planning and implementation stage, is the tendency for the problem to change or evolve into a new and different problem — or a *secondary problem*. In other words, things rarely work out as planned, or things can be planned only up to a certain point beyond which new problems arise and new decisions have to be made. When new problems arise, the lawyer has to renew the problem-solving process. The lawyer has to re-examine the goals, gather new facts, identify issues, develop and evaluate new options, and modify plans.

Aside from seeing problem-solving as a linear process of stages, therefore, lawyers should see it as a fluid process — either as a process of continual renewal as new problems arise, or as one requiring modifications as they move through the stages. Though presenting the problem-solving model as a linear process of stages is helpful in providing a logical step-by-step method for problem-solving, it is equally important to include the concept of fluidity, which emphasises flexible thinking and the ability to identify new or unforeseen problems which may emerge during the stages. For example, if you were to proceed through the stages, new problems inevitably come up, and you have to be flexible and ready to move back and forth among the various stages to ensure that goals, facts, issues and options have been fully explored; or you might have to reorder the stages in order to meet individual circumstances; or you might have to restart the process entirely.

So while the linear aspect of the model can provide you with a step-by-step method for solving problems, the flexibility aspect should help you appreciate the complexity of problem-solving. The legal problem-solving process should always be treated as a living, changing process (see Figure 3-4).

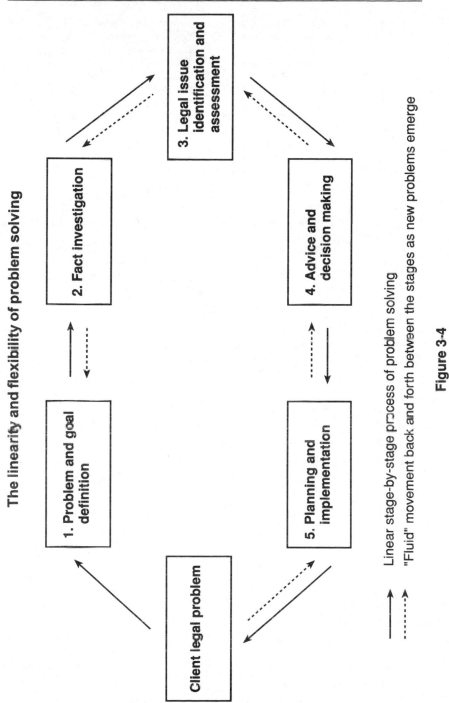

The linearity and flexibility of problem solving

1. Problem and goal definition

2. Fact investigation

3. Legal issue identification and assessment

4. Advice and decision making

5. Planning and implementation

Client legal problem

Linear stage-by-stage process of problem solving

"Fluid" movement back and forth between the stages as new problems emerge

Figure 3-4

[1] Some of the material for this chapter is adapted from Stephen Nathanson, "The Role of Problem Solving in Legal Education" (1989) 39 *Journal of Legal Education* pp.167–183 and "Problem Solving in Professional Legal Education" (1989) 2 *Journal of Professional Legal Education*, pp.121–140.

[2] See, for example, Andrew Leigh, *Decisions, Decisions: A Practical Management Guide to Problem-Solving and Decision-Making* (Gower Publishing Company, Hampshire, 1983), Chap. 1; and K.F. Jackson, *The Art of Solving Problems* (Heinemann, London, 1975); John F. Vinsonhaler, Christian C. Wagner and Arthur S. Elstein, *The Inquiry Theory: An Information-Processing Approach To Clinical Problem-Solving Research and Application* (East Lansing, Michigan, 1978), p.20.

[3] See, *e.g.* Russell Stewart, *Curriculum Development For The Practical Legal Training Course* (Centre For Legal Information and Publications, Sydney, 1979), pp.77–78.

[4] See, *e.g.* Carrie Menkel-Meadow, *Toward Another View of Legal Negotiation: The Structure of Problem Solving* (1984) 31 UCLA Law Review 754 at 804

[5] See Andrew Leigh, *Decisions, Decisions*, *op. cit.,* p.65

[6] Gary Bellow and Bea Moulton, *The Lawyering Process: Negotiation* (The Foundation Press Inc., Mineola, NY, 1981) pp.50–55.

[7] David A. Binder, Susan C. Price, *Legal Interviewing and Counselling: A Client-Centred Approach* (West Publishing Co., St. Paul, Minn. 1977), pp.147–155.

[8] D. Rosenthal, *Lawyer and Client: Who's In Charge?*, as reprinted in Leonard L. Riskin and James E. Wesbrook, *Dispute Resolution and Lawyers*, (West Publishing Co., St Paul, Minn., 1987), p.74.

[9] *ibid* at 74–75.

[10] James Freund, *Lawyering: A Realistic Approach to Legal Practice* (Law Journal Seminars-Press Inc., New York, 1977) pp.268–279.

[11] In relation to civil proceedings see, *e.g.* E.T. Horne, *Corderey On Solicitors* (Butterworths, London and Edinburgh, 8th ed., 1988), p.50.

[12] See, *e.g. The Supreme Court Practice* (Sweet & Maxwell, London, 1997), Vol. 1, Part 1 (Rules of the Supreme Court) and Vol. 2, Part 2 (Forms).

CHAPTER 4

LAW SCHOOL THINKING AND LAWYER THINKING

Although problem-solving concepts may seem disconnected from present-day undergraduate legal education, meeting points between them do exist. To help students see the relevance of what they learn in law school to legal problem solving, this chapter examines the relationship between the two and the ways in which they fit together as well as diverge.

LAWYER IMAGES AND LEGAL EDUCATION

When students start studying law one of the first classes is usually in contract law. The teacher might begin with the topic of how contracts are made and points out that this occurs when an offer is made by an offeror and is accepted by an offeree. The teacher might illustrate the point with the famous case of *Carlill v. Carbolic Smoke Ball Co.*[1] which is always intriguing to the newly initiated.

Students might begin to read the recommended text on contracts to learn about legal concepts — consideration, repudiation, discharge, breach, remedies — and cases which illustrate these concepts. Some students might, during periods of reflection, start to wonder how the topic of contract law relates to what lawyers actually do or to the lawyer images with which they are familiar. What, for example, is the link between this subject and what the characters in *L.A. Law* do? The students may struggle to make connections. They may try to imagine how lawyers in real life deal with contracts by referring to their own experience. Even non-lawyers know or have heard, for instance, that lawyers draft contracts to try "to cover all the angles" and that the documents contain "fine print" and "legalistic language", but that lawyers analysing them sometimes find "loopholes". They know that people "breach" contracts and that lawyers sue them for "damages".

In other words, before people start law school, many have already had experience of contracts, if only second-hand. It is natural that they would want to relate what they learn in law classes to that experience. To grasp the subject, students might thumb through a textbook on contracts looking for concrete examples of written contracts. They might think by seeing a real contract drafted by a practising lawyer, the subject might be easier to learn. But most textbooks on contracts do not contain examples.

They contain organised summaries of legal concepts and cases, but not practical examples of contracts.

An equally vain search awaits someone who tries to find a connection between criminal law and the variety of criminal-lawyer images to which they have been exposed. The subject of criminal law and criminal-law textbooks offer little guidance on how to prepare a criminal defence or how to address a jury with a powerful closing argument. Those hoping that the techniques of someone like Rumpole will be revealed in the course or that they will be taught how to avoid the mistakes Atticus Finch made are likely to be disappointed.

Instead of learning the principles of conducting a defence (or prosecution) of criminal defendants, most students spend their time memorising concepts such as *actus reus* and *mens rea* and analysing how they are viewed by judges. Teachers explain these principles and review the way judges interpret them. Discussions sometimes follow about why judges have different interpretations. In other classes, a factual scenario may be presented and students asked to identify legal issues as well as to argue for one side or both, or even to predict what a judge might decide with those facts.

What about *torts*? Most students have some kind of prior knowledge of tort law. They know that lawyers who specialise in it act for people who have been injured, usually in motor vehicle accidents. They know that aggressive personal injury lawyers can win vast sums for injured clients. They have seen tort cases portrayed in films such as *The Verdict* and on television. In law school, however, the curriculum is often dissociated from this prior knowledge. From the curriculum, students learn that torts are non-contractual wrongs and negligence is the most common of these wrongs. They study cases on negligence similar to those on *mens rea*. A torts teacher may present bizarre scenarios such as, what if someone throws a ball out the window and it causes a boy on a bicycle to fall into a puddle, as a result of which he catches a cold that turns into pneumonia from which he dies? What were the causes of his death? Was his death reasonably foreseeable? Can his parents bring legal action? The learning methods are similar to other subjects; the cases are reviewed and the judgments studied.

The most famous of these cases is probably *Donoghue v. Stevenson*.[2] Students may read what the House of Lords had to say, but they may never learn the most significant thing about *Donoghue v. Stevenson* — how the plaintiff's lawyers broke new ground in this case. They probably will not learn the lessons of how to prepare and win a difficult tort case. In most tort law classes, the connection between tort law and practising law is not clearly established for students.

It is similar in the teaching of the law of real property, which can appear even more mystifying. Students know from experience that real property is important. People build their homes on it. It is the largest investment in most people's lives. Why then, students might ask, is so much emphasis placed on topics such as *fee tail*, *reversionary interests* and *remaindermen*? The language of real property law is particularly arcane, bound up with history, ancient statutes, and the common law.

Lawyers clearly have to work with real property, but students may find it is difficult to connect the law of real property with their ideas about what lawyers do. A typical real-property book may mention that the law of real property is important to lawyers in relation to facilitating the transfer of property. It also might say that the main purpose of learning real-property law is to support the study of conveyancing. But then conveyancing is hardly mentioned in the rest of the book. To the students, the law of real property may seem truly removed from real life.

Why study contracts without examples of contracts? Why study criminal law without learning how to defend criminals, or tort law without learning how to sue a wrongdoer, or property law without learning how to transfer property? The answers lie in how legal education has evolved, in the history of legal education: despite recent changes that have brought more courses relevant to legal practice into the curriculum, many law schools still provide an educational regime that focuses mainly on law, is not sufficiently connected to real life, and does not include enough about practice. The history of legal education is not the subject of this book, but the issue needs to be raised so that students can understand present-day legal education and its limitations. One of the limitations students need to understand is that what they learn in law school is based on *law school thinking*, which is quite different from *lawyer thinking*. Lawyer thinking is different in scope, depth and viewpoint.

LAW STUDENT THINKING

One of the more important questions asked by law teachers is, where does law come from? Or, what are the sources of law? In the English system, though the law may originate from legislation, common law or equitable principles, it is the judges who interpret the law after hearing evidence and arguments presented by lawyers. Their interpretations are written down in judgments which, when well-written, are helpful in explaining how the law applies to specific situations. From the reader's point of view, these judgments can be intriguing, because they contain reasoned decisions about how to resolve conflicts between real people. They are certainly more interesting than legislation which is boring to read; judgments are also more interesting and complex than bare statements of legal principles. Because of this, law teachers consider judgments an important source of law and the primary medium through which they convey legal principles to students.

Not surprisingly, law school thinking is strongly influenced by these judgments and by the many books and articles that law teachers write about them. The main result of this influence is to focus thinking not on clients' legal problems, but on legal issues that judges have to resolve. The principal problem considered in many law school classes is similar to what lawyers do when they make a prediction assessment: in other words, given a set of facts, which legal issues applied in what way will determine the outcome in front of an intelligent judge?

Students, like judges, look at both sides of legal issues and at conflicting issues. As a result of this kind of educational shaping, the structure of law students' thinking is like that of appeal-court judges. Students do not think like trial court judges because they are not asked to make decisions about witness credibility or the weight of evidence. They are taught to focus on legal issues and how to resolve them as do appeal-court judges; they are not often taught to focus on the client's problem and how to solve it.

Many examinations reinforce, and also narrow, this structure of thinking. Though classroom time may be spent in identifying and applying legal issues as well as predicting court outcomes, because of time pressure examinations tend to test the students' ability to identify legal issues at the expense of application and prediction. Fact patterns in examinations are frequently unrealistic, imbedded with many issues students are called upon to identify. The more issues students identify and explain, the higher their scores will be. In its most elemental form, law school thinking calls for issue-spotting. The law student's basic strategy for learning law in this environment is first, to memorise as many legal issues as possible and secondly, to practise spotting them in old examination papers. Learning to think this way will probably improve performance in law school, but does not do enough to train students to be competent lawyers.

LAWYER THINKING AND PROBLEM SOLVING

If law teachers concentrate on teaching legal issues and the lawyers of popular culture concentrate on the big questions of truth and justice, what are real lawyers concerned with? The answer is, clients' legal problems. How would the average law student perform in handling real-life legal problems? Let us first look at an example of a simple legal problem (based on actual events) and analyse the ways a law student and a lawyer might approach it:

The problem — commercial tenancy

Your client is the owner of retail premises in a bustling area of the city. He has been looking for a commercial tenant for these premises and has just found one. A prospective tenant, Alan, offered him £1,500 per month for two years in a letter setting out the tenancy terms in detail. The client and Alan signed this letter which says at the top "subject to contract". Two days later the client notified you that he has found another tenant who is prepared to pay £1,800 per month for the first year and £2,000 per month in the second year. The client, who wants to enter into a contract with the new tenant, sends you a fax with a copy of the letter, asking for immediate advice about what to do.

A law student given this kind of problem is trained to identify and analyse the legal issues. Since this problem is a real one, not many legal issues arise. The main legal issue is this: does the letter constitute a binding, enforceable contract? Or, do the controversial words "subject to contract" render it unenforceable? If it is unenforceable, the client is free to enter into the contract with the new tenant.

For the lawyer, the first issue would not be enforceability, but to identify the nature of the problem. The lawyer needs to define the problem to make sense of it. After careful preliminary investigation of the facts, including a close examination of the letter, the lawyer would try to define the problem.

One of the most direct ways to define a problem, as we have learned, is to identify the client's goals: what does the client need or want? What risks is the client prepared to assume in getting there? Does he really want the extra money no matter what the risk? Is he prepared to assume the risk of litigation whether or not his lawyer gives a favourable opinion on the issue of enforceability? Is he concerned about the effect on his reputation should he decide to repudiate the first contract?

As things turned out, the client was unconcerned about his reputation. After careful questioning, he indicated that, as far as he was concerned, if the lawyer's opinion was that the contract was *probably* unenforceable, he was prepared to repudiate it immediately. He wanted the higher rent. What he was somewhat concerned about, however, was the possibility of litigation as well as the cost and time involved. He was only prepared to risk litigation if he thought he had a really strong case on enforceability. But he wanted the case to be so strong that the prospective tenant would be unlikely to sue him.

How did the lawyer in this case actually define this problem? After questioning the client she ascertained that the client's goal was to get more money out of the premises than he had agreed to and he wanted to achieve that goal with a minimum of legal risk.

What did the lawyer advise? She made a rough prediction assessment that the contract was arguably unenforceable and so advised her client. Then she outlined a plan to the client that he contact Alan personally to inform him of his lawyer's advice, and the new offer he had received. After gauging Alan's reaction, he should then consider renegotiating the rent. She felt that a lawyer's direct involvement would only formalise the conflict, inflame the parties and harden positions.

The advice worked well for this client. Alan was annoyed, but apparently relieved to be given the opportunity to renegotiate. He also sought advice from his own lawyer who must have told him there were arguments to be made on both sides of the issue. The two parties quickly settled on a rent of £1,800 for two years. The client's goals were met and the problem solved to his satisfaction.

In this process of *problem solving*, the legal issue of whether or not there was an enforceable contract was not the problem; it was only a part of the problem. The lawyer's opinion on this issue and the way she viewed it (the contract being arguably unenforceable) led to an assessment of the legal risk of repudiation: if the client repudiated, the client *might* win if sued. It was this assessment of legal risk that shaped the lawyer's approach to the problem. She devised a way of minimising risk even further by suggesting direct negotiation between the client and Alan without lawyer intervention.

Playing out conflict

This commercial tenancy problem involves a conflict that requires resolution. I have called this a *playing-out conflict* problem. Problems of this type are not always resolved peacefully; they may sometimes involve tactical moves designed to defeat opponents in litigation. The identification and analysis of legal issues is an important part of problem solving in playing-out situations. In the commercial tenancy case, the identification and analysis of the legal issue led to an *assessment* of legal risk. The result of the assessment helped to shape the lawyer's advice and the client's decision-making.

The identification and analysis of legal issues is used in other ways in solving playing-out conflict problems. It also plays a role in the *investigation of facts*. In the commercial tenancy case, after the lawyer identifies enforceability as the key issue, she can investigate the facts further by examining the letter more closely or questioning her client. She might look for more evidence relating to enforceability. She can find out why the words "subject to contract" were used. She will undoubtedly explore what the parties' intentions were at the time the letter was signed and what other language in the letter is relevant to the issue of enforceability.

We can see even from this simple case how complex lawyer thinking is when compared with law school thinking. Yet we can also see a relationship between the two types of thinking. The identification of legal issues (law school thinking) is but one stage in the process of realistic legal problem solving (lawyer thinking). (See Figure 4-1.)

In the shoplifting case that Rumpole was defending, the legal issue was *mens rea*, or guilty mind; that is, did Rumpole's client have the intention to steal the merchandise? Law students looking at this issue would try to identify the circumstances that indicate a guilty mind and compare them to circumstances found in other similar cases. Through this process of reasoning they might reach a conclusion about whether *mens rea* is proved beyond a reasonable doubt.

But for Rumpole, bristling with hostile energy, the problem was how to play out the conflict so that the jury would believe his client did not have a guilty mind. One of Rumpole's strategies in solving this problem was to arouse the English jurors' dislike of unhelpful shop clerks. He used this strategy when cross-examining the store detective by suggesting that the shop clerk was so unmindful of the needs of shoppers that his client was forced to try to pay for his purchase on another floor.

The foundation of most effective cross-examination is to use questions to advance the theory of the case.[3] It matters little what the witness' answers are; what matters is the content of the questions and the way they are put. Rumpole applied this principle in his cross-examination. The legal issue, *mens rea*, was obvious; Rumpole's problem was to devise a strategy for showing the client did not have it. In essence, the strategy was to make this argument: "you're saying my client's behaviour showed a guilty mind; well, you're mistaken. He did what he did because of lazy shop clerks with whom everyone is familiar." Rumpole's cross-examination, carefully thought out, advanced this theory. It could be said that Rumpole, in his lawyer-thinking way solved the problem, not by identifying *mens rea* as an issue, but by proving the lack of it in his client.

Blocking conflict

Now let us consider a different sort of problem and examine how a law student and a lawyer might view it:

The problem: separation agreement

Your client is a woman who has negotiated a separation agreement with her husband who is now living with another woman. Their only major asset is a house that is owned equally (*i.e.* as joint tenants) by both of them. The wife has a well-paying job and the husband has his own small business. They have agreed to an amicable settlement to sell the house, split the proceeds, give the custody of the child to the wife, reasonable access to the husband and arrange maintenance payments for the child of $750 per month. The wife wants you to draw up the separation agreement and she wants your legal advice.

Many law students might look at this problem and ask, where's the problem? One simple issue is, given the couple's respective incomes and the child's needs, is $750 per month an appropriate amount? But the lawyer could go well beyond this issue. Having established that the amount is appropriate, his or her thinking would then be influenced by other factors. For example, lawyers know that people — especially estranged husbands — sometimes breach agreements. So the lawyer would carefully question the wife to ascertain the likelihood of the husband keeping up his child maintenance payments. The higher the risk of breach, the more likely it is that the lawyer might try to persuade the client to structure the separation agreement a different way.

For example, if the lawyer determines that the situation is risky for the wife, he or she might suggest the house not be sold until the child is much older and that the husband's half-interest be used as security for the maintenance. If the husband does not agree to this, the lawyer might suggest that less maintenance be paid as long as that maintenance is effectively secured. Another suggestion might be that the wife agree to a transfer of the husband's half-interest in full satisfaction of her claim for maintenance. Through a process of interviewing and advising, and negotiating with the husband or his lawyer, and drafting the agreement, the wife's lawyer would solve the problem of how to structure the agreement. A great deal is at stake here because a vague, poorly structured agreement can cause conflict to occur and trust to deteriorate.

To meet the client's goal, which is to ensure her husband shares the responsibility of maintaining the child, the lawyer should draft provisions that express the literal intentions of the parties. Most important, he or she needs to anticipate future conflicts and structure the agreement so as to *block* them. The lawyer might block them by negotiating and drafting an agreement that gives her the house and releases the husband from his maintenance obligations, or by securing the husband's maintenance obligations against his half-interest or, perhaps, in some other way.

Furthermore, in drafting various provisions, the lawyer should ensure that the language and structure make the agreement — and any necessary supporting documents — impervious to legal challenge. For example, if the maintenance obligation is to be secured against the husband's half-interest in the house, the lawyer must ensure that correctly-worded provisions are inserted, that relevant security documents are signed and that the arrangements agreed to will, if tested in court, be approved by it. The lawyer is minimising legal risk — the risk of a legal dispute flaring up, and the risk of being on the losing side even if it does — by taking effective blocking action.

This problem is the other kind that lawyers confront. It has been called a *conflict-blocking* problem because solving it involves a process of decision-making that seeks to realise client goals by minimising legal risk through blocking potential conflict. This type of problem solving is also related to law school thinking. Law school thinking focuses on developing the students' ability to identify legal issues in a factual scenario and to predict the success of arguments on both sides of the issue. With conflict-blocking problems, however, predicted success in relation to one side or another of an issue is usually not critical. What is critical is whether or not a conflict might arise and whether or not the other side can maintain a credible position arguing their case. The lawyer's task is to create a list of these potential conflicts and to use various documents and procedures to block them. Taken together, these documents and procedures are what we have referred to as *plans* (see Figure 3-3).

The conflict-blocking lawyer has a lower profile than that of the conflict player and so, perhaps, has a less controversial, more benign image. Since the conflict-blocker's job is to prevent rather than play out conflict, it is only natural that he or she has a more benign image. Legal conflicts are costly — not only in time and money but in the amount of human misery they can cause. Clients who are sophisticated and understand the unhappiness that legal conflict brings appreciate this type of legal work. They like agreements and documents that are "airtight", that have no "loopholes", and that stand the "test of time". The conflict blocker is not a law-warrior. He or she is a law-maker, legislating private agreements and documents for and between people who need control over, and clarity in, their lives.

Even clients who are relatively unsophisticated appreciate the benefits that competent conflict blockers can bring to a situation. Anyone who has ever had a close relative who has died without a will, or with a poorly-drafted will, knows how much acrimony can be caused

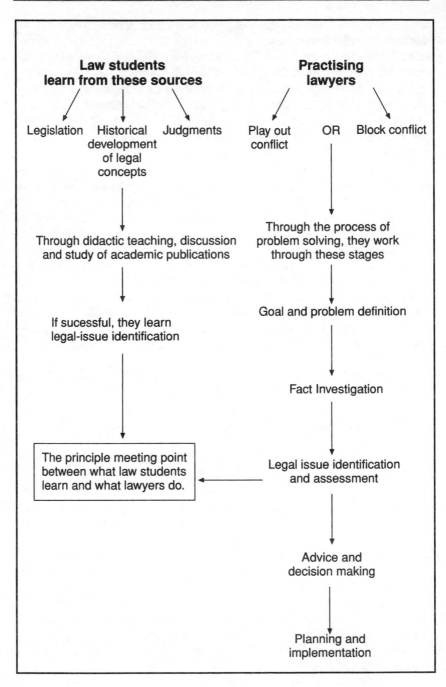

Figure 4-1

when different people have different interpretations of what the deceased's intentions really were. When the lawyer does not get things right, when there is confusion about who is entitled to what, brothers and sisters can end up bitter for a long time.

On the other hand, a lawyer who knows how to draft a will competently, and advise a client how he or she should dispose of property to avoid disputes will certainly help that client and the family to avoid the heartache that can result when an estate is drained by litigants and their lawyers.

The role played by conflict-blocking lawyers is one of the least understood and most neglected in law schools. Law schools spend much of their time on sources of law such as judgments and legislation, but the one source that probably produces more law than any other is overlooked. That source is conflict-blocking lawyers who are engaged in the enterprise of law-making. This, of course, is not the law-making that goes on in legislatures or the courts, although it is related to these sources. This is the vast enterprise of law-making that goes on every day in lawyers' offices and in the legal departments of thousands of firms: the creation of private law accomplished through the negotiation and drafting of agreements and transactions that govern legal relations between people.

[1] [1893] 1 Q.B. 256.
[2] [1932] A.C. 562.
[3] Michael Hyam, *Advocacy Skills* (Blackstone Press, London, 1992), p.84.

CHAPTER 5

PLAYING OUT CONFLICT: THEORY AND PRACTICE

WINNING VERSUS SETTLING: THE MAIN PROBLEM

Unlike conflict-blockers, lawyers who play out conflicts, particularly courtroom hero and warrior types, are familiar to the public. The heroes are mostly the stuff of fiction, but in the internationally televised O.J. Simpson trial, the public had an opportunity to see real legal warriors in action.

Simpson, an African-American football hero and media star, charged with the murder of his wife and her friend, was defended by a team of brilliant and fierce defence attorneys who used a variety of strategies to show the mostly African-American jury their client had reasonable doubt in his favour. Simpson did not testify and there were no eyewitnesses or confession to the murder. Though strong, all the evidence was circumstantial. Simpson's blood was found at the crime scene; traces of blood which contained the victim's and Simpson's DNA were found in his vehicle, at the crime scene, and on a pair of socks found in his home. A bloody glove which matched the one found at the crime scene was found on Simpson's estate. Embroiled in a marital relationship filled with conflict, Simpson appeared to have a motive for murder.

His lawyers' strategy was to establish an alibi and to hold every piece of circumstantial evidence under a microscope. This was done through vigorous cross-examination of witnesses, as well as with the help of forensic specialists who cast doubt on police evidence-gathering techniques and laboratory procedures.

As the trial unfolded, the defence team demonstrated the importance of flexible thinking. They modified their strategy. Alibi evidence the defence intended to introduce turned out to be flimsy, so they dropped it. Instead, they focused on the physical evidence and Mark Fuhrman, one of the investigating detectives who collected some of the evidence. On cross-examination, F.Lee Bailey from Simpson's defence team, accused Fuhrman of feeling antagonism towards African-Americans and using the word "nigger", (referred to as the "n" word throughout the trial). He also accused Fuhrman of planting the bloody glove on Simpson's estate. Fuhrman emphatically denied these accusations.

Rare is the case that a policeman is caught red-handed lying on the witness stand. Unfortunately for Fuhrman and the prosecution's case, however, the defence proved him to be an outrageous liar and a racist. It appeared that, prior to trial, Fuhrman had been interviewed and taped by a screenwriter who was researching a story about the Los Angeles police. On the tapes, he used the "n" word repeatedly and boasted of manufacturing evidence in other cases. The defence succeeded in getting excerpts of the tapes into evidence and that was the end of Detective Fuhrman's credibility.

The lead counsel in Simpson's team, Johnny Cochran, a lawyer with exceptional oratorical skills went on the offensive blasting the Los Angeles police in his closing remarks before the jury. "This man is an unspeakable disgrace", Cochran told the jury of Fuhrman. He also accused the prosecutors of putting Fuhrman on the stand knowing he was a liar. "They made him seem like a choirboy.... they knew he was a liar and a racist." In a dramatic finale to the day's presentation, Cochran accused Fuhrman of planting the bloody glove on the Simpson estate.

The following day he continued his impassioned plea to the jury, comparing Fuhrman to Adolf Hitler and suggested that convicting Simpson would signal a victory for racism in America. Cochran detailed what he said was a vast conspiracy led by a "lying genocidal racist" cop to frame Simpson for a crime he did not commit.[1]

Strong words? Perhaps not. Cochran's strategy needs to be viewed in context. In America, divisions between races run deep. Most African-American people confront racism on a daily basis and view the police as front-line deliverers of racial injustice. To the jurors, nine of whom were African-American, most of whom have undoubtedly witnessed or experienced police harassment at some time in their lives, Cochran's appeal appears to have touched their sense of injustice.

But let us now examine briefly whether, despite his outstanding courtroom victory, Cochran's strategy was good for his client. At the outset, in dealing with the O.J. Simpson case Cochran might have defined the problem like this: what do you do when the evidence is overwhelmingly against the client? Cochran's solution is reminiscent of the story about the great advocate who, when asked to explain his courtroom success to a class of law students, said, "When the facts are against me I hammer the law; when the law is against me I hammer the facts." "What happens," asked a law student, "when both the facts and the law are against you?" "I hammer the table," he replied.

Cochran's strategy was as heavy-handed as any table-hammering harangue, but no less effective for it. All he had to do was persuade one juror that Fuhrman's racism destroyed his credibility and that this would sufficiently taint the evidence to create reasonable doubt. The result would be at least a hung jury.

Many people were appalled by Cochran's strategy, and affronted by his demagogic appeal to racial grievance. Even one of Simpson's own lawyers, Robert Shapiro, distanced himself from Cochran's strategy. But Cochran was a conflict player and, like all the players in this conflict, he was playing to win. The rules and the judge allowed him to play that way and he did. In an adversarial system, lawyers need not care whether the public approves or disapproves. What counts is solving their client's problem by choosing the best strategy for winning. As one prosecution witness, who had just undergone a devastating cross-examination, said of a defence lawyer: that's his job, he gets paid for it.

The jury in the Simpson case obviously responded to Cochran's appeal. Against the predictions of all the pundits, most of whom predicted a lengthy deliberation and a hung jury, the jury took less than four hours to come up with an acquittal. As Robert Frost once said, "A jury consists of 12 persons chosen to decide who has the better lawyer." The defence strategy was so powerful and Cochran's oratory so persuasive, that even in the face of strong evidence of guilt, the jury was prepared to have reasonable doubt.

Because the trial was such a publicised event and an anomaly, it may be difficult to draw too many conclusions from it, but one lesson is clear: with superb courtroom skills and unlimited resources, a lawyer can work wonders when he or she adopts the right strategy.

But what if, from the beginning, this case had taken a different turn? Suppose Simpson had instructed his lawyers that he would consider pleading guilty to a lesser charge and that they should negotiate with the prosecutors on his behalf for a lighter sentence. In this scenario, the client's goals would be different and so the problem would be defined differently: it would not be how to get an acquittal in the face of strong evidence, but how to attract the lightest sentence possible.

If, for the sake of argument, Cochran could have negotiated, but advised his client not to, then one could say he put his client through an unnecessarily tortuous ordeal and enormous expense, as well as risking two consecutive life sentences on conviction for first degree murder.

One could also argue that Simpson got more than he bargained for by going to trial. The publicity surrounding it has made him a pariah. It is likely that society at large will revile Simpson and he will be an outcast forever. The case may not only have left justice unresolved but Simpson's life as well. Perhaps Cochran's choice of strategy and his focus on winning may turn out to be less beneficial to his client in the long run than it might seem at first glance.

On the other hand, winning and knowing how to win are critical skills for a courtroom lawyer. Once a trial has been lost, it is a rare lawyer who can convince the client that all is not lost. Even in negotiations, a reputation for winning is important because your adversary knows that if negotiations break down, a tough fight is in the offing. As Rex Carr, a high-profile Illinois trial lawyer specialising in personal injury cases, says, "I frequently get more money in settlements than I believe I can get in a trial. Some insurance companies hear my name and they say, pay him what he wants. They are fools to do that. But they believe in my reputation and they pay." [2]

Lawyers like Mr Carr recognise the importance of having a winning reputation. A colleague of his who later became Chief Justice of the Illinois Supreme Court once suggested to him that a poor settlement has its benefits because it minimises the risks and stresses of a trial. But Mr Carr viewed it differently: "A poor trial is better than a good settlement, because I've gotten all my business from publicity about me and my cases. You don't get publicity from a settlement. Nobody even hears about it — nobody but me and my client."[3]

To be a responsible professional, however, the conflict player needs to know when not to try a case, how to settle, and how to help the client reach a settlement and feel satisfied about it. In playing-out conflict situations, settling and winning are two sides of the same coin. The most critical point in any lawsuit, after negotiations have occurred and an offer is made, is whether to continue the lawsuit or accept the offer. The decision is always a big one because clients seeking justice have a large emotional investment in their quest.

To most clients, when they first hire a lawyer, justice does not mean compromise or settlement; it means vindication, exoneration or victory. As lawyers guide them through the process of playing out conflict, most clients quickly learn that going to court can result in not getting justice and that this can be financially and psychologically ruinous. Lawyers in playing-out conflict situations are dealing in a world of intense emotions and big risks.

Mr Carr, the lawyer with the winning reputation, took an enormous gamble acting on behalf of a number of plaintiffs in a toxic-tort case, known as *Kemner v. Monsanto*. Carr sued a railroad and a chemical company, Monsanto, for damages to his clients (who included the Kemners) as a result of a dioxin spill in a small Missouri town. Carr asked for $12 million to settle the case. Since he had already received $5 million in settlements in related litigation, that left $7 million still to be extracted.

Carr was surprised when the railroad offered him the unexpectedly large sum of $4 million. He decided to change his strategy. His main target had always been Monsanto and with $4 million already on the table from the railroad, he assumed he had been too easy on Monsanto. This is where he made a crucial error. He withdrew his initial demand

and came up with a new demand of $9 million to Monsanto alone. Monsanto became intransigent and refused to negotiate further. Carr also made the mistake of not spreading his risk by accepting the railroad's offer of $4 million. He took the whole matter to trial.

After a marathon 44 months before a jury, and a closing argument in which Carr asked for over $35 million, the jury awarded each of the plaintiffs a token $1 dollar. The Kemners received $29,000 because their land was damaged by the dioxin spill.[4] The lesson to be learned from this case is that the flip side of playing to win is that sometimes you lose.

LEGAL PROBLEM SOLVING: MAIN AND SECONDARY PROBLEMS

The lawyer's basic strategy for playing out conflict is to meet the client's goals by winning or settling to the client's satisfaction. How this is to be achieved depends on the lawyer's competence.

On the road to solving the client's main problem, the lawyer has to solve many secondary problems. The process is not unlike a perilous journey one has undertaken. The lawyer's job is like that of a guide leading the client through hostile, often unpredictable, territory. Having made similar journeys before, the lawyer knows the terrain and the rules to follow. But rules are always open to interpretation and nothing is certain until settlement or final judgment. Until the journey's end, ambiguity and uncertainty enshroud the process, causing stress to both client and lawyer.

The following is a real case that illustrates the challenges of problem solving in a conflict-playing situation.

The case: Gallo v. Fornelli

(Names and details have been altered to preserve confidentiality.)

The Litigants

Mr Gallo is in conflict with old friend and business partner, Mr Fornelli. They were both Italian-Canadians who had grown up together in Italy, and emigrated to Canada at the same time. In their youth they were very close, but then went their separate ways when they became adults. Mr Gallo eventually left for the United States, where he became an American citizen, living in Florida. In the early part of 1985, he returned to Vancouver to discuss a business deal with his old friend, Fornelli, who saw opportunities in the Vancouver property market.

The Deal

Fornelli suggested putting joint capital into buying houses to sell later at a profit. Gallo agreed that it was a good time to speculate on the Vancouver property market, so he went into partnership on a 50:50 basis with his old friend. They would put 10 per cent down and finance the balance with a mortgage. Gallo, who was returning to the United States, left all the business and legal details to Fornelli and handed over C$30,000 as his share of the deposit for the purchase of properties. They agreed that the properties and the mortgage were to be registered in Fornelli's name alone.

The Events

With the joint capital, Fornelli bought two identical houses adjacent to one another in 1985 in the West End of Vancouver. He found tenants for them, collecting rent which did not quite cover the mortgage payments and expenses. In 1987, Fornelli tried but failed to sell the two houses at their original price when the Vancouver property market was in the doldrums. He continued to rent the houses out while his secretary sent Gallo unsigned notes on Fornelli's company stationery outlining contributions for mortgage payments and other expenses that Gallo was required to pay. Gallo sent cheques to Fornelli to cover these expenses.

In 1991, Fornelli substantially increased the rents on the houses, and his secretary also stopped sending Gallo demands for contributions. Gallo assumed that by that time the rental income received covered the mortgage payments and other expenses and that profits were minimal. He thought that Fornelli had kept whatever surplus might be available to put towards maintenance of the two houses.

The Problem

Mr Gallo returned to Canada in January 1994 to discover that house prices in Vancouver had shot up and the two houses were worth five times their original 1985 price. He then tried to contact Fornelli to sell the houses, but Fornelli avoided him, not taking his telephone calls or always being out of the office. On the one occasion he managed to reach him, Fornelli refused to discuss the houses. Mr Gallo decided to consult a lawyer, Angela Tate.

As with all good lawyers, Ms Tate needed to get beyond the obvious. She needed to understand the litigants and their conflict. Ms Tate describes how she proceeded to define the main and secondary problems and the process she engaged in to deal with them.

Goal and problem-definition: "After Gallo came in and told his story, it was clear to me that he just wanted his half interest in those houses and he did not want to have anything more to do with Fornelli. He already had some experience of litigation in the United States, and wanted to sue right away. He did not even want me to write a letter of demand or one opening up negotiations. He was so anxious to get moving, he asked my secretary how much I would want as a retainer. He definitely wanted quick action; he did not want to be dragged into a lengthy proceeding. He was constantly travelling and lived so far away that he did not want to have to return to Canada periodically to give me instructions.

I was concerned about a number of problems. The most immediate one was, did Fornelli still own the houses or did he have any money out of which we could secure any judgment — if we were fortunate enough to get one? Another problem was why was Fornelli acting in this way? What made him think he could succeed in depriving Gallo of his interest in those houses? I thought it was extremely important to ascertain his reasons because this would give me an insight into both the strength of the opposition's case and, perhaps, the strategy he would adopt to defend it. This, in turn, was related to the most basic problem, which was would we have difficulty proving Gallo was entitled to a one-half interest in the two houses?"

Fact investigation: "I spent several hours with Gallo on two separate days to make sure I understood all aspects of the story. The first day I got the outlines of it and looked closely at the documents which were voluminous and in a mess. Although they confirmed his story, only two or three of them had Fornelli's handwriting on them, and no signature. I started thinking about evidentiary problems and questioned my client about the secretary who had prepared the earlier documents, but he had never met her. He had no idea where she might be and could not remember her name. I got his instructions to hire a detective to trace her, if necessary. This was because I wanted to find her myself rather than through a formal discovery process which would alert Fornelli that I was looking for his secretary.

The first day, I also did a Land Title search to find out about the two houses, as well as any other properties Fornelli might own, and it turned up some interesting results. He had sold one of the two houses for C$500,000 in 1992. He then mortgaged the remaining house and two other properties he had purchased on his own. The mortgage which covered those three properties was a collateral mortgage used to secure a banking facility for Fornelli's business. The limit of the facility was C$1,000,000. Of course, there was no telling from the documents I looked at how high that facility had gone. The sale of one of the houses, the purchase of the two other properties and the establishment of the new mortgage arrangements all took place around the time Fornelli stopped sending my client the demands for mortgage contributions.

When I discussed these search results with my client, the reasons why Fornelli had been avoiding him and resisting his claim started to became clearer. He had used the houses to finance his business and possibly the acquisition of other property. Perhaps, I suggested, he was not really intent on resisting the claim forever; maybe he was just intending to delay it to keep his business going.

My client did not agree with me about this. His theory was Fornelli had just got used to the idea the houses were his and did not want to part with them. In his view, Fornelli was a thief.

I started to dig more deeply. Why, I asked, did you not tell Fornelli to register the houses in both your names when you agreed to the investment? I suspected my client was hiding assets from somebody, perhaps a wife or creditor. As it turned out I was close to being right because he was engaged in a little bit of tax shenanigans. He had made all payments for the houses out of his company account and had characterised these as corporate tax-deductible expenses.

After hearing this, I concluded Fornelli had assumed that my client was unlikely to sue him for fear that the tax authorities would discover his scheme. But my client said he was so aggrieved he did not care about being reported to the IRS. Besides, he was confident his accountant could help him deal with the IRS if that became necessary."

Legal-issue identification: "As my investigations proceeded, I was thinking about the line of legal attack I would take. It is most important in a situation like this, where the opposition is capable of getting rid of property swiftly, to tie up whatever property he does have to prevent him from selling or mortgaging it.

I could do this under British Columbia law by pleading that my client had an equitable interest in those properties and then by filing a *lis pendens* against them in the Land Title Office. He certainly could claim he had an equitable interest in the original two houses because he could show he had contributed money directly to their purchase and maintenance. Perhaps he could also prove an equitable interest in the later two properties that Fornelli bought on his own, if we could prove that cash from the first house that was sold was used to purchase the other two properties or to maintain them.

My plan was to allege this first and gamble that we could prove it later. At any rate, this was a typical case of *constructive trust* in which you plead in the statement of claim that the defendant, although legal owner of the property, holds some or all of it on trust for the plaintiff.

I quickly drafted the statement of claim saying that the plaintiff was entitled to a half interest in all three properties 'or such interest as the Court may declare after an accounting...'. On the basis of these documents filed in the Court Registry, I could then file a *lis pendens* at the Land Title Office against the properties thus preventing them from being sold or mortgaged further. I also pleaded breach of an oral agreement by Fornelli and alleged substantial damages. I completed all this on the second day, hired the private investigator to look for the secretary. My client left Vancouver that evening."

Advice and decision-making: "When we served Fornelli with the writ and statement of claim, he hired a lawyer and denied everything. The defence he filed was quite weak, however, and he made no mention of a counterclaim for unlawful filing of the *lis pendens*. I therefore assumed that he might very well have used the sale proceeds from the first house to buy the later two properties.

In the meantime, the detective found the secretary, but she refused to give a statement to him and claimed she could not remember the documents he showed her. She said she had not worked for Fornelli for many years.

I now had to consider where to go from there. I had a stack of documents that appeared to show a pattern of payments consistent with the alleged agreement, but no indisputable evidence that proved the agreement between my client and Fornelli. I felt that Fornelli was just playing for time. Maybe he had reasoned that the houses were his because my client had appeared to lose interest in them and he, Fornelli, had done all the work while my client had just sat back waiting for the profits to roll in. Perhaps, Fornelli might have thought, even if Gallo did have an interest, he was entitled to delay since Gallo had done nothing to assert his claim for many years. It was important for me to find Fornelli's motive and predict what his strategy might be.

After all, the issue as I saw it at this stage was strategic and, if Fornelli's *modus operandi* was to delay, then he did not intend to see the matter through to trial. If this was the case, I needed to apply pressure and do something that would bring the matter to a quick conclusion, such as the filing of a summary-judgment application.

Since my client did not want to wait years for trial and did not have the time to keep flying back to Vancouver to give instructions, he agreed to my recommendation to attempt a summary-judgment application.

Nevertheless, we had a problem. Under the rules for summary judgment you need very strong evidence to succeed. And the evidence must be contained in the documents; oral evidence and cross-examination are not permitted. In our case, there was a stack of documents for the court to wade through and, although the evidence in my view was very strong, I thought that an effective advocate for Fornelli could exploit ambiguities in our documents and sow seeds of doubt in the judge.

I explained to my client the rules for summary judgment. We could file an affidavit, I explained, and produce all the documents, but they could file an affidavit too. Since there was no opportunity to cross-examine, any false allegations they made in their affidavit would be very difficult to disprove. The summary-judgment application might then be dismissed with costs awarded against my client. The entire exercise might well cost him several thousand dollars.

My client asked me what the chances of success were and, on the basis of my knowledge of various judges, I said we had a 50 per cent chance of success. He gave me instructions to go ahead."

Planning and implementation: "I had a fine day in court on the day of the application. It was just after the summer vacation started; not many people were around and the judge had lots of time to read the documents before he heard our submissions. Fornelli had filed a contradictory affidavit basically denying everything, but saying he had no recollection of a specific agreement made in relation to the houses, although they may have had a "general understanding" that Gallo would be entitled to some of the profit on sale if he kept up the payments. However, Fornelli swore that my client lost interest in the houses during the market doldrums in 1987 and stopped sending any more money. Fornelli recollected that he spoke once to my client on the telephone. He claimed my client said he considered the whole investment to be a "write-off" and that Fornelli could do what he wanted with the houses. Furthermore, Fornelli swore he could not remember who sent my client the demands for mortgage contributions on his company stationery.

Although my first reaction was to believe that this confusing affidavit might be enough to raise a doubt in the judge's mind, the judge seemed unimpressed with it. I had pointed out to him that the lack of an explanation on the use of Fornelli's business stationery to record the financial dealings was a fundamental weakness in

Fornelli's case. The judge agreed. He also wanted to know the specific terms of the "general understanding" alleged by Fornelli and he gave Fornelli's lawyer one week to come up with them in a supplementary affidavit, as well as an explanation for why Fornelli's secretary sent Gallo statements on the company's stationery, detailing the need for mortgage and other contributions from 1985 to 1991.

When we returned to court one week later, Fornelli's lawyer tried to get an adjournment saying he was unable to get his client's instructions, but he did not give any reasons why. The judge rejected his request and gave summary judgment in my client's favour.

But the judgment was only a general declaration that my client was entitled to an interest in all three properties and that the defendant was a constructive trustee. We still needed to have a full accounting to determine the extent of that interest. We hired an accountant, as did the defendant, to go through all the papers to summarise their respective contributions to the properties. The defendant's accounts, needless to say, produced results miles apart from ours.

Meanwhile we estimated it would take a three-day court hearing to resolve the issue and we could not schedule that hearing for at least another nine months. I suggested to Fornelli's lawyer that we resolve the matter by appointing an accountant as a mediator, but Fornelli would not agree to this or even to open up negotiations."

Advice and decision-making (repeat stage): "One of the options was just to wait for the hearing and prepare thoroughly for it. The other was to apply pressure which my client was keen to do. So I suggested we write a letter to the bank that held the mortgage on the three properties, informing it about the judgment and suggesting that, because of my client's interest in the properties, the bank should advance no further money to Fornelli or his company.

I explained to my client that this was quite a risky move. I had no idea of the state of Fornelli's business affairs or of what the consequences of that letter might be. The bank probably already knew about the lawsuit, but banks are skittish organisations. Suppose the bank decided to call in all the indebtedness? One or more properties might be foreclosed, Fornelli's business might fold and he, as well as my client, could end up with nothing.

Furthermore, I said, there was a possibility we might both be sued by Fornelli if it turned out later that the scope of my client's interest was really quite minimal.

But my client really liked the idea. He wanted to do it despite the risks. He even started to reassure me and give me legal advice. Don't worry, he said, you won't get sued. Fornelli's father just died and left him a lot of money and property in Italy. He'll never allow that business to collapse or the properties to be foreclosed."

Planning and implementation (repeat stage): "I resolved to go ahead. I prepared a draft of the letter to the bank informing them of the judgment and explaining in some detail its implications. I suggested that the bank should not advance further money to Fornelli or his company. I then discussed the strategy and the letter with a senior colleague in our firm. He was all in favour of sending it out except that he suggested that I fax a draft to Gallo with a covering letter outlining the risks, and obtain his written instruction to send it. I followed this suggestion because I could see how it would clarify the advice I had given and confirm the client's instructions.

We sent the letter to the bank and nothing happened for a month. But then something in my letter to the bank (I had given them a copy of the judgment as well) triggered their concern and they started foreclosure proceedings. That really worried me so I called Gallo. He told me not to worry: Fornelli was quite capable of refinancing or even paying off the indebtedness.

The same day I spoke to Gallo on the telephone, Fornelli's lawyer called and asked for a meeting at my office. He wanted to sit down and discuss the whole matter. Naturally I agreed, subject to my client's approval.

When Fornelli and his lawyer arrived at my office, I was struck by how unwell Fornelli looked: he was quite obese, his face was pale and puffy and he was chain-smoking. He appeared to be in a state of barely controlled rage and looked as if he was going to have a stroke. My office is a smoke-free zone, but I let him smoke.

As it turned out, I think my client might have exaggerated the extent of Fornelli's financial resources. Fornelli said he could not pay off the mortgages or refinance. I half-believed him. Obviously, there was a lot of pressure on him. His lawyer accused me of legal extortion. He said, you already have a *lis pendens* and a judgment. Why did you have to write to the bank? They did not know about the legal action until you alerted them. It's just pressure for its own sake.

After I brushed aside these accusations, we began negotiating and did not conclude until the next day. We went back and forth, and I was on and off the telephone with my client. It became evident to me that my client's expectations had risen. In addition to his initial investment and the returns on it, my client wanted to get even. His first offer, which he stuck to until the end of the first day of negotiations, was that he wanted the original house that had not been sold (clear title), half of all profits from the accumulated rents, plus interest on the profits, all his legal fees paid, and a written apology.

I suggested that he drop the demand for the apology, but he refused. When I put the offer to Fornelli, I could see his face darken when I mentioned the written apology. He appeared very agitated and rejected the offer outright.

I telephoned Gallo from another office and told him that if he did not withdraw the demand for an apology, our strategy could backfire — Fornelli could get stubborn, fall ill or die; his business could collapse. My client might get nothing out of it. He listened, but then asked what Fornelli looked like during the negotiation. When I said he was chain-smoking and seemed on the verge of having a stroke, he wanted more details.

I could tell Gallo was feeling triumphant from my description so I continued talking about how ill and defeated Fornelli looked. I did not discourage my client from feeling satisfied, but did remind him gently and repeatedly that putting Fornelli in a wheelchair or into his grave would not help him get his money.

After a while, my client softened his stance. He gave me carte blanche to settle on terms I thought were fair. When I returned to my room, Fornelli and his lawyer were just about to go. 'Mr Fornelli is tired', his lawyer said. So I immediately offered to go to the lawyer's office the next day, suggesting that my client was going to make a significant concession. They agreed.

The next day we settled on what I thought were reasonable terms. Fornelli agreed to pay off half of the business loan from his own resources and by selling one of the other properties. Subject to the bank's agreement, the business loan would then be refinanced without using the original house as security. That house, which would then be clear of encumbrances, was to be sold. Ninety per cent of the proceeds would go to my client and ten per cent would go directly to the bank to reduce the mortgage further and induce the bank to agree to the arrangement. Gallo would waive all claims to the accumulated rents and interest, and neither party would have any further claim against each other.

Several months later the house was sold, the agreement put into effect and the Gallo/ Fornelli dispute ended. Looking back on that case now I can see the main problem more clearly. I could not see it at the start, but came to understand it as the matter proceeded. Fornelli had rationalised that the two houses were his, because he had done all the work and my client had not been around to help. Then when my client started to stake his claim years later, Fornelli procrastinated and delayed, hoping somehow that my client would go away. My problem was how to convince Fornelli that Gallo was serious, wanted his share, and would persist with his claim until it was satisfied."

This is the way Ms Tate, with the benefit of hindsight, viewed the problem — the main problem of winning or settling to the client's satisfaction. It shows that the process of problem solving, and the problem itself, is a dynamic one. It changes as the problem unfolds and as problems are solved or new problems crop up. At one point, the problem was proving the constructive trust, but that was solved by effective fact-investigation and advocacy. The problem evolved into one of proving with accounting records the size of the trust. But because Fornelli was a procrastinator and his strategy was to delay, the problem became how to avoid having to prove the size of the trust in a lengthy accounting hearing many months hence. Then that turned into how to pressure Fornelli into coming to the negotiating table. And then, during the negotiation, Ms Tate did not want to undermine her gains by pushing Fornelli so hard that he refused to compromise; so the next problem was how to induce him to come to terms while controlling her own client's urge to hurt Fornelli. Lastly, the problem of structuring the settlement agreement had to be addressed; its main feature was to take account not only of the parties' goals but the bank's as well. Prompted by Ms Tate's negotiating finesse, Fornelli agreed to refinance his business loan from his own resources and channel his share of the house proceeds directly to the bank. (The outlines of the problem-solving process she followed are illustrated in Figure 5-1.)

These were all secondary problems Ms Tate needed to solve before she could tackle the main problem of winning or settling. Ms Tate solved the secondary problems by working through standard procedures in a linear way ensuring, for example, that fact-investigation, legal-issue identification and the implementation of plans proceeded in an orderly way. She also needed to be flexible and quick-thinking as, for example, when she fed her client's need to hear about Fornelli's anguish during the negotiations, when she solved the problem of how to short-circuit the waiting time for an accounting hearing and when she structured the settlement agreement with Fornelli's lawyer. During this process she played out the conflict with both winning and peaceful resolution in mind. A lawyer can make both winning moves and moves to resolve the conflict by negotiation in order to maximise options for the client.

As for Ms Tate's handling of the opposition, most players would agree that it is not advisable at the beginning of a conflict to make overtly peaceful moves. Some research even exists that suggests a co-operative stance is more likely to elicit a positive response if it is preceded by an aggressive one.[5] There is some evidence to suggest that Ms Tate's

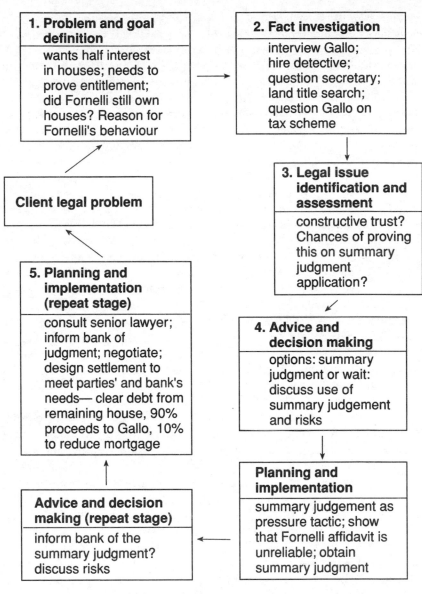

Figure 5-1

A problem-solving process: Gallo v. Fornelli

The evolution of one problem into another is depicted by repeating the advice & decision-making and planning and implementation stages.

decisive and timely handling of the various problems that cropped up was very competent indeed. It is safe to assume that if she had not started and pressed legal action, had not brought summary-judgment proceedings and had not written that letter to the bank, Fornelli's lawyer would not have asked to negotiate.

Ms Tate's handling of her own client was also skilful. Had she not convinced her client to stop trying to destroy Fornelli, the negotiation might never have succeeded. As Ms Tate worked through the main problem and secondary problems arose, she handled them with a mixture of caution, boldness and flexibility.

---

[1] Material on the O.J. Simpson Trial is drawn from Elizabeth Hardwick, *Family Values, Vol. XL111, No. 10, The New York Review of Books*, (June 6, 1996) 7 at pp.9–10, *The South China Morning Post,* Friday, September 29, 1995, *Clear "Framed" OJ, Jury Urged* (Reuters)

[2] John L. Jenkins, *The Litigators*, (Doubleday, New York), pp.350–351.

[3] *ibid.*

[4] *ibid*, p.350.

[5] Gary Bellow and Bea Moulton, *The Lawyering Process: Negotiation* (Foundation Press, Mineola, New York, 1981), p.156.

CHAPTER 6

THE PLAYING-OUT CONFLICT PROCESS

In the last chapter, we looked at the problem-solving process from start to finish in a specific playing-out situation. This chapter looks at playing-out conflict more generally. It also modifies the process model and focuses on key aspects of each of the stages. Since playing out conflict is all about settling or winning, the process can be modified to reveal a sequence of four stages that move it toward its settling or winning goals: 1. identifying the legal issues; 2. investigating the facts; 3. negotiation and 4. advocacy. (Figure 6-1 at the end of this chapter outlines the sequence.)

1. IDENTIFYING LEGAL ISSUES: DEFINING LEGAL WRONGS

Legal rights and wrongs

When a client wants to enforce or defend legal rights, a legal conflict follows. The concept of legal rights has challenged legal philosophers for centuries, and much of the law student's time is devoted to studying how rights come into being and what they really are. While the idea of legal rights is helpful to conflict players, it is probably more common for them to think in terms of *legal wrongs*. This is because when clients seek a lawyer's advice they do not usually know what their rights are, but they certainly know when they feel wronged or have been unjustly accused of committing a wrong. The lawyer listens to their stories of injustice and tries to ascertain whether a legal wrong has been committed.

If the lawyer sees that it is likely that a legal wrong has been done, he or she can advise that legal action be commenced. One of the lawyer's first steps in the attack is usually to threaten the other side with legal action, and if a threatening letter is not enough, the lawyer then writes up the situation in a formal way so that it discloses that a legal wrong has been done. This legal wrong, such as a tort or breach of contract, is set out in the form of pleadings. For a prosecutor in a criminal case, the legal accusation may be set out in an indictment. To succeed in a trial, the lawyer must prove the facts of the accusation and demonstrate that they do indeed constitute a legal wrong.

If the client is the one accused of a legal wrong, the lawyer will listen to a different kind of story but one that requires him or her to do essentially the same job in reverse: demonstrate that no legal wrong has occurred through the defence and other pre-trial manoeuvres. If the action goes to trial, the lawyer will try to attack the accuser's evidence and prove the worth of his or her own case.

Known wrongs and new wrongs

Defining legal wrongs or setting up defences to them is usually one of the first big problems with which the conflict player has to contend. If the facts fit easily into well-known categories of wrongs or defences, the lawyer's job is easy. But when they do not, the lawyer needs to think up new wrongs or defences as well as clever variations of known ones. Conflict players have been doing this to help their clients for a long time. In a real sense, the history of the common law is a history of conflict players trying to get justice for their clients by stretching the categories of known wrongs and making up new ones.

With its roots in medieval England, the common law was much more formalistic than it is today. Plaintiffs claiming wrongs had been done to them had to bring a separate "form of action" for each known category of wrong. Each form of action required a different writ and a different procedure. If the wrong form of action was used, even if the claim had merit, it could be thrown out. At one time only one form of action at a time could be used; plaintiffs could not sue in the alternative. Rules of pleading were strict and could easily result in injustice. Moreover, if a wrong was done and it was not covered by any of the forms of action, redress was difficult, if not impossible.

The law progressed, however, presumably through the work of creative conflict players acting on behalf of injured clients. A form of action called *action on the case* developed. This form of action was more flexible and permitted lawyers to bring more experimental actions, eventually expanding the scope of legal wrongs. Lawyers developed ways of drafting pleadings to bring them within the action on the case. As new types of claims became established, lawyers could fit their actions safely into these new categories. Finally, in the nineteenth century forms of action were abolished and uniform procedures for all actions were introduced in the High Court.[1]

The lawyer's job of fitting actions into known legal categories, and developing new ones did not end with the abolition of forms of action. It continues in legal practice to this day, reflecting both the linear and flexible aspects of legal problem solving. The linear aspect involves using precedent pleadings and modifying them so that the facts fit in to known categories. For example, in a straightforward personal injury case where the client has suffered injury in a motor vehicle accident, precedent pleadings can be used to insert the key facts, describe the defendant's negligence, detail the type and scope of injury and quantify some or all of the damages to the plaintiff.

Sometimes, however, the facts do not fit known legal rules, yet the client's injuries and distress call for justice. Though not as constrained by forms of action as their predecessors, contemporary lawyers still work in a rule-of-law environment, basing their client's case on existing laws, but reinterpreting them so fact and law somehow fit. Or, acting for a civil or criminal defendant, they may have to reinterpret facts so they fall outside the breach of law of which their client is accused. In these situations, legal problem solving demands varying degrees of ingenuity. Take this example:

A lawyer was making a bail application on behalf of his drug-addict client. The prosecution opposed bail (unless stringent conditions were imposed) on the principle that the accused was unlikely to show up for trial because he had fled from the scene and because the crime with which he was charged was serious. According to the prosecution, the arresting police officer saw the accused engaged in what appeared to be a drug transaction with another known addict. The officer recognised the accused because he had arrested him twice previously on suspicion of drug trafficking. The accused, however, had not been charged with any crimes and had no criminal record. When the accused noticed the officer approaching, both he and the other addict fled. One of them, the officer could not see which, dropped a bag on the roadside which later turned out to contain 20 grammes of heroin — an amount more than enough to warrant a trafficking charge. Both of them were later arrested and each said the other had dropped the bag and that no transaction had taken place.

On a bail application, one of the rules is that the burden of proof is on the prosecution to show why the accused should not get bail or should get bail but with stringent conditions. The wrong alleged by the prosecution was that the accused fled the scene, a sure sign he did not intend to show up for trial. A lay person looking at this situation would probably say that the accused had done sufficient wrong fleeing from the scene to justify stringent bail conditions and, given the other facts, to satisfy the prosecution's burden. But the accused's lawyer used ingenuity to demonstrate that his client's behaviour was both explainable and unrelated to an intention to avoid trial: the reason he fled was simply because he recognised the police officer and did not want to be arrested by him again! According to the accused's lawyer, the accused had not done anything wrong and fully intended to show up for trial, because he knew that with the facts presented by the prosecution, he had an excellent chance of acquittal.

In the law reports one can find many examples of lawyers using ingenuity to define legal wrongs or defend accusations. Although it is the judges who record the lawyers' arguments in the law reports and get the credit for original thinking in deciding cases, it is usually the lawyers who have developed those arguments.

The classic case of *Carlill v. Carbolic Smoke Ball Company*,[2] decided at the end of the nineteenth century, illustrates the point. The defendants, owners of a medicinal preparation called the "Carbolic Smoke Ball," published an advertisement in which they offered to pay £100 to anyone who used their smoke balls in a prescribed way, and still caught influenza. Mrs Carlill, the plaintiff, relying on the advertisement, used the preparation as prescribed and caught influenza. When the defendant refused to pay the £100, she sued for it.

At that time, no legislation existed that could protect purchasers of patent medicines from false advertising, so the plaintiff's lawyers had to define a wrong based on existing law. They made an ingenious argument. They said the advertisement and Mrs Carlill's subsequent purchase of the product constituted a contract and that the defendant's failure to pay was a breach of contract. The defendants' lawyers, equally ingenious, argued that you cannot make a contract with the whole world, *i.e.* readers of the advertisement. But then, the plaintiffs' lawyers pointed out that a contract was not made with the whole world. An *offer* was made to the whole world and the plaintiff, by buying the smoke balls and using them as directed, accepted it. Offer and acceptance resulted in the formation of a contract.

Mrs Carlill's lawyers had stretched the boundaries of contract law so that Mrs Carlill's performance of the conditions constituted "accept-ance." The judges in the case approved. As A.W.B. Simpson says, the judges "fictitiously extended the concept of acceptance to cover the facts".[3] The reverberations from this judgment have had a profound effect on legal education. Since 1893, "law students have been introduced to the mysteries of the unilateral contract through the vehicle of *Carlill v. Carbolic Smoke Ball Co.* and taught to repeat, as a sort of magical incantation of contract law, that in the case of unilateral contracts performance of the act specified in the offer constitutes acceptance, and need not be communicated to the offeror".[4] The result may have been an illogical twist in the law of contract, but that is what can happen when lawyers think creatively to get justice for their clients.

Creatively defining legal wrongs does not depend on ingenuity alone. It also requires other ingredients. In one of the best known cases of the common law world, *Donoghue v. Stevenson*,[5] lawyers demonstrated how with persistence, courage and superb advocacy skill, the tort of negligence could be redefined.

Donoghue v. Stevenson, like *Carbolic Smoke Ball*, was a case involving consumer protection and product liability in the 1930s before these areas were developed as distinct legal subjects. As almost every law student knows, the plaintiff in this case, Mrs Donoghue, drank ginger beer out of a bottle she subsequently learned had a decomposed snail in it. She became seriously ill and sued the manufacturer for negligence. The defendant's lawyers made an application to have the plaintiff's claim dismissed on the ground that it disclosed no cause of action: that is, even if the plaintiff could prove everything in her claim, no legal wrong was done, because the defendant did not owe the plaintiff any duty of care. The application was taken all the way to the House of Lords, the defendant's lawyers arguing that under negligence law, as it then was, only certain categories of relationships between people created duties of care. Manufacturers, they argued, did not owe a duty to consumers apart from contract (there was no contract between Mrs Donoghue and the manufacturer) or unless the situation fitted into certain exceptions, such as when the manufacturer knows the articles are dangerous.

To the contemporary law student, even to the modern lay person, this argument sounds ludicrous: of course, manufacturers owe a duty of care to the consumer. But in 1931, two of the five law lords, Buckmaster and Tomlin, on the basis of the law as it then was, were justified in disagreeing. In an era when consumers' rights were not yet well-established, their Lordships did not think much of the plaintiff's lawyers' attempt to stretch the manufacturer's duty of care too widely.

Fortunately for the plaintiffs, however, the other three law lords, led by Lord Atkin, agreed with plaintiff's counsel. Lord Atkin, in giving his reasons for judgment, came up with the much praised "neighbour principle". He injected into tort law the Christian principle "love thy neighbour", transforming it into the rule that people should take care not to injure their neighbours.

Law teachers and legal texts throughout the common law world have praised Lord Atkin's judgment for changing tort law. The following is an example of what they have written:

> "This is undoubtedly the most important tort case decided in the twentieth century... As a result the law moved closer to the moralist's idea of negligence. The expansion of the duty of care, on the authority of Lord Atkin's general principle, ultimately led to the position that a duty of care is almost always owed in relation to negligently caused personal injuries, death and property damage".[6]

Another legal text has gone beyond this claiming, for example, that the transformation of the love thy neighbour principle into negligence law is a glorious idea reflecting the creative power of both tort law and the common law generally.[7]

Although these remarks have the advantage of adding an inspiring dimension to the study of tort law, they hardly present a full picture of the dynamics underlying creativity in the common law. Though it is true that courts can be creative, the innovative thinking process is usually generated by lawyers who, with ingenuity, energy and sheer doggedness, fight to get justice for their clients.

In the House of Lords, the barristers arguing for Mrs Donoghue, evidently demonstrated these qualities. They spent two days delivering their argument.[8] The plaintiff's counsel (George Morton K.C. and W.R. Milligan) argued that although there was no clear precedent to support the existence of a duty of care in this case, there was no clear precedent against it either. In this particular case, the manufacturer's duty should not be strictly limited: "When a manufacturer puts upon a market an article intended for human consumption in a form which precludes the possibility of an examination of the article [*e.g.* ginger beer in a sealed bottle] he is liable to the consumer for not taking reasonable care to see that the article is not injurious to health".[9]

Although they used American law to support their argument, Morton and Milligan must be credited with solving the problem of defining a new legal wrong at that time. They did a first-rate job for Mrs Donoghue, and were obviously heedless of how much money they were going to make. Mrs Donoghue was so impoverished she had to petition the House of Lords to prosecute her appeal *in forma pauperis*. Indeed, she swore in her supporting affidavit that she was not "worth five pounds in all the world."[10]

Finally — and to fill in the picture — much of the credit must go to Mrs Donoghue's solicitor, Mr Leechman, who not only took on her unfortunate case, but went all the way to the House of Lords with it. A measure of both her suffering as well as her solicitor's skill in describing it is revealed in an extract from Mr Leechman's written pleading on her behalf:

"She suffered from sickness and nausea which persisted. Her condition became worse, and on August 29, 1928 she had to consult a doctor. She was then suffering from gastro-enteritis induced by the snail-infected ginger beer. Even while under medical attention she still became worse and on September 16 had to receive emergency treatment at the Glasgow Royal Infirmary. She vomited repeatedly, and suffered from acute pain in the stomach and mental depression.

She was rendered unfit for employment. She has lost wages and incurred expense as the result of her said illness."[11]

Mr Leechman was courageous and persistent. He had just lost two similar cases on appeal to the Court of Sessions. In each of these he had proved a ginger beer bottle had a mouse in it, but in keeping with the law at that time, negligence was not proved.[12] Leechman was undaunted by these losses — losses that must have meant a tremendous amount of time and money lost. At that point, many other solicitors would have said to themselves: no more animal-in-the-bottle cases for me. Amazingly, however, less than three weeks after he lost the second mouse appeal, Leechman was at it again, issuing Mrs Donoghue's writ.[13] Leechman, knowing the precedents were against him, was still intent on defining a new legal wrong so his client could get some justice. And he was prepared to go all the way to the House of Lords to do it.

The most instructive thing about both the *Donoghue* and *Carbolic Smoke Ball* cases is not how the judges decided them but how their lawyers got them into court in the first place.

2. INVESTIGATING THE FACTS

In law school, it is probably true that no topic is more neglected than *fact investigation*. Students can learn the skills of negotiation, interviewing, drafting, writing and advocacy through techniques such as simulation; but except in clinical courses in which students practise investigating facts under supervision, very little about fact investigation is taught in law schools.

This is understandable since designing courses so that students can simulate the investigation of facts would be an expensive endeavour. Nevertheless, law students must be aware of the critical importance of fact investigation in legal problem solving. Once more, this perspective on the legal process is probably at odds with the experience of many law students who are taught to focus on law rather than facts. But cases are built on both facts and law working together. And as the conflict moves toward trial, facts often loom larger. The outcomes of trials depend on how the judge or jury sees the facts and, in many cases, the two sides will present different versions of key events. Naturally, how those facts emerge depends to a great extent on the lawyer's skills in identifying, gathering and organising them. Even if a conflict is resolved before trial through negotiation, the positions that lawyers take and their decisions on settlement depend on perceptions of facts that have been gathered.[14]

Facts can be gathered from many sources — from interviews with people (clients and witnesses), from documents, photographs, maps, site visits, and examinations of actual objects or real evidence. I shall deal briefly with two of the most common sources, people and documents.

Getting the facts from people

The procedures involved in getting facts from people are many and varied. Interviewing the client and interviewing witnesses are two such procedures. Interviewing witnesses presents different problems from interviewing clients. For example, witnesses may be reluctant to provide information for fear of becoming involved in a legal conflict, whereas clients may be too eager to provide unhelpful rather than helpful information.

To overcome witness reluctance, lawyers need to identify first the reasons for the reluctance and to discuss and explore these as a way of developing rapport.[15] With clients who ramble on, providing unhelpful information, lawyers can use simple techniques such as interrupting clients to get them to focus or reminding them how the right information can help their case get back on track.

Getting the facts from people involves a variety of skills such as effective questioning and listening, understanding how the facts and the law are related, and techniques for identifying and responding to feelings. Some law students view interpersonal skills, sometimes called *soft skills*, as being unimportant to the practice of law, and as getting in the way of learning the hard skills of legal problem solving.[16] This belief sometimes exists among law students who have had little experience of client contact or interacting with people in a professional or other formal setting and fail to see how important these skills are. Unfortunately, this belief is given further credence by some courses in legal interviewing that focus too heavily on interpersonal skills, and not enough on the skills of legal analysis and advising. Legal interviewing courses need to be crafted carefully to balance the teaching of effective interpersonal skills and legal problem solving.

If students do not have the opportunity in law school to learn the interpersonal skills they need to get facts from people, they should at least try to remember how important those skills are. Perhaps one way is to remember the lesson learned by the lawyer in this anecdote:

"I was acting for a woman in a custody case against her husband. The custody of a young boy was in question. An older boy was in his twenties and living on his own overseas. I had done a lot of preparation on the case and the more I learned about the father, the more I didn't like him, but our evidence was wishy-washy. One problem was that the psychologists' reports were vague and indecisive. They did not come down in favour of one parent or the other. Both reports, however, did say my client had been receiving psychiatric help for anxiety and depression for many years. She was passive, meek and unassertive. So the reports hurt us more than they helped us. The husband's strategy was typical: he wanted to demonstrate his wife was crazy, get the boy away from her, and thus minimise his financial liability to her.

There wasn't really anything I could pin on her husband. He was very quiet at home, one of those cruel, cold, quiet types. Because he was so quiet, it was hard to get any concrete evidence of speech or behaviour to reveal the kind of man he really was. One day in a meeting with my client and my secretary I became frustrated at not being able to come up with stronger evidence, and I blurted out, 'What are we going to do with this heartless bastard!' At my comment, my client turned beet red and averted her eyes.

A few weeks passed. My client brought some documents into the office. She was accompanied by her older son who had just returned from Europe. He wanted to know how the case was going. We started to converse and I asked him a few open-ended questions. Suddenly he said, 'Did mother tell you what he does in front of us to show his opinion of her cooking?'

'No,' I said.

'As soon as the food's on the table, he puts it on the floor for the dogs to eat and then takes us out for pizza.'

The son then proceeded to provide a few other examples of the husband's disrespectful behaviour. I suddenly felt I had a much stronger case. When I asked my client why she hadn't told me all this before, she changed the subject.

Later, my secretary gave me an insight into both my client and myself: 'She heard you speak contemptuously of her husband. She didn't want to tell you the pizza story because she thought you would think even worse of her for being such a doormat.'

I won that case and learned a valuable lesson: it is all right for a client to speak contemptuously of his or her spouse, but the lawyer should refrain from doing the same."

In this case, the lawyer's judgmental comment caused the client to become inhibited about revealing intimate, highly relevant facts about the marriage. Only the good fortune of meeting her son had saved the lawyer and his client from presenting a weak case in court. The real lesson here is that with the acquisition of effective interpersonal skills, such as being non-judgmental and knowing how to establish rapport, a lawyer can get at the facts of the case more efficiently.

Getting facts from documents

In Dicken's *Bleak House*, the image of lawyer as paper generator overwhelming the legal system with documents fails to take account of the important role conflict-players assume as document investigators and analysts. Documents are usually the lifeblood of civil cases. They often contain the key, or at least the clues, to solving playing-out problems. One can get the facts from documents simply by reading them carefully. The following anecdote from a lawyer illustrates the importance of studying the paperwork carefully:

"I was acting for a truck driver in a personal injury case. It was a garden-variety whiplash. Client was rear-ended. He complained about neck and back pain and losing time off work. He brought in a big pile of documents — pay slips, claim forms, medical reports, physiotherapy reports, a messy diary and so forth. I read and organised them, noticing that he had made a previous whiplash claim and had received $7,600. We discussed this and he explained that it had occurred four years ago and he had completely recovered. I asked him if he had made any other claims and he said 'no'. I got the file going, started legal action, and notified the defendant's insurer.

The insurer's solicitors were quite a good firm, whose style was to make frequent settlement offers on PI claims to get them turned over quickly and keep legal bills down to a minimum. They made me an offer of $12,000 almost immediately after the pleadings closed and paid that amount into court. I advised my client to take it. I thought it was a decent offer. I explained that if he didn't accept it and we went to court and the judge awarded damages of $12,000 or less, he would have to pay all of the defendant's legal costs from the date the payment into court was made. That was quite a big risk, but he refused to settle.

A year later we went to trial. During my client's cross-examination, he admitted to the previous whiplash claim and the $7,600 settlement. Then counsel dropped a bombshell. 'Did you make yet another similar claim five months after you made the first one?' Counsel then produced a claim form with my client's signature on it. I looked through my document bundle to find the form and sure enough, a copy of it was there. I had had it all along. The insurer's solicitor had given me a copy in discovery. But it was so similar in form and content to the first form, and so close in time, I had assumed — wrongly, of course — that it was simply another form filled out for the same claim.

But then I looked at it more closely and I noticed it had a different claim number! It was another claim for another accident and, to the

court, it must have made my client look like a con man. My heart sank
and so did my client's credibility. His case collapsed. I considered
myself lucky when the court was decent enough to award him $2,800
even though it was not enough to pay the defendant's costs."

This particular document was provided by the opposite party during
the *discovery* process. In civil cases discovery occurs after the pleadings
are closed and both sides are obliged to make available to each other all
relevant documents. Sometimes there are disputes about what is
relevant. Other times one party may feel relevant documents are being
withheld or concealed and applications to court can be made to try to
flush them out. Getting your hands on the right documents can often
make your case or break the other side's. But whatever documents you
do get hold of, whether provided by your client or through discovery,
they must be carefully scrutinised.

The fact is, people really do reveal themselves in documents and,
sometimes, all it takes is a careful reading of readily available
documents to come up with the most damning evidence. The famous
multi-billion dollar asbestos litigation of the 1960s, 1970s and 1980s, in
which thousands of American asbestos workers sued companies such as
Johns-Manville and Raybestos-Manhatten for exposing them to fatal
doses of asbestos dust, is a stunning case in point. At the beginning of the
conflict, the corporate defendants dug their heels in, their lawyers
pleading that their clients were not aware of the deleterious effects of
asbestos until about 1964. This defence would enable them to avoid
multi-million dollar claims for punitive damages flowing from conspiracy and fraudulent concealment, knowingly exposing employees to
hazardous asbestos dust and covering up what they knew about its toxic
effects.

In April of 1975, Karl Asch, a New Jersey attorney representing
several hundred asbestos workers, was sitting at home reading the 1974
Annual Report of Raybestos-Manhatten, a leading asbestos manufacturer. He came across this passage in the report:

"For many years [since 1930], it has been known that prolonged
inhalation of asbestos dust by factory workers could lead to disease.
...In addition to pioneering the design of engineering controls,
Raysbestos-Manhatten joined with other asbestos products manufacturers in the mid-1930s in funding long-range research programs on
the biological effects of asbestos. Because of the long latent period of
asbestos-related disease, the disease being found today among some
industry employees is a result of conditions existing decades ago

when little was known about the health effects of asbestos or proper means of control."

Asch was struck by the blatant contradiction in the report. Rays-bestos-Manhatten had always maintained that that it did not know of the deleterious effects of asbestos until the 1960's. But the self-congrat-ulatory words in the Annual Report showed it clearly knew of those effects since the 1930s. Asch's more than 200 clients, many sick and dying, had never once seen a warning label on any of the bags of raw asbestos they had to work with when employed; yet here was the same employer boasting not only that it knew of the dangers but had commissioned research into it decades before.

The information in this report, published by the defendant company and available to the public, led Asch into discovering a great deal of other incriminating documents which helped him and other attorneys bring lawsuits against the asbestos makers. This set the stage for an avalanche of asbestos litigation, which involved billions of dollars in damages for the hapless victims.[17]

3. NEGOTIATION

Once litigation gets underway, the parties to the conflict usually look for ways to resolve it other than trial. They do not always communicate their intention to their adversaries, but they do look for opportunities to attempt settlement. Although alternative methods of settlement such as mediation are becoming increasingly popular and effective, the most common method is still negotiation.

For anyone trying to learn negotiation in the context of the playing-out-conflict process, it must first be understood as a stage in that process. As a stage, it builds on the first two stages, *identifying legal issues* (defining legal wrongs) and *investigating the facts* (see Figure 6-1). Once this is grasped, competent negotiation can then be viewed as requiring two basic ingredients: *knowing the law* and *knowing the facts*.

One of the best illustrations of this claim is contained in a brilliant video vignette created by Gary Bellow and Jeanne Kettleson for the American Bar Association.[18] In the video, the scene opens with a young lawyer named Beach working in his office. He is representing a couple named Valdez whose son was killed in a car accident. They are suing Alloway's Garage alleging that its mechanics negligently failed to tighten the lug nuts on the wheels of their car. The wheel collapsed and their son was killed.[19]

Beach's investigator, Eads, enters the scene to find out whether Beach wants further investigation done. Eads seems to feel that the mechanic,

Rossini, should be questioned further. Rossini has already given a deposition (a sworn statement) denying any wrongdoing. Beach does not want to pursue the investigation. He thinks the case is a loser.

"Naw...", says Beach to Eads, "forget it. We already got his deposition. I mean, I don't want you to put any more time into this. I can't afford to put any research into this either.....the case is a dead loser.....[it's] not worth more than...ah...five thou[sand] at best."

The scene soon shifts to Beach meeting with his clients, Mr and Mrs Valdez. They are grief-stricken over the loss of their son. The little boy had not been wearing his seat belt when the accident occurred. This failure to wear a seat belt constitutes contributory negligence and Beach advises them it presents a serious legal obstacle to recovery.

In the next scene, we see Mr Kepler, an obviously competent and highly experienced, if somewhat ethically borderline, lawyer dictating a confidential memo to his file. In the memo he notes that Beach is probably unaware that the accident occurred immediately after the introduction of a new negligence statute, the practical effect of which was to eradicate the seat belt issue as a legal obstacle to recovery. He also notes in the memo that Rossini, the mechanic, has changed the story he gave earlier in his deposition. Rossini now admits that the Valdezes really did ask for a full inspection of their car, but that it was not done. Kepler wants to settle quickly before Beach finds out about the new negligence statute and before he has an opportunity to unearth facts that Rossini concealed in his deposition. Kepler's insurance company client has authorised him to settle for $20,000.

In the next scene, Beach and Kepler are negotiating. Kepler offers to pay only medical expenses of $2,000. Here Beach's glaring lack of preparation on both law and facts proves to be his undoing:

Beach: Look, I know we've got a problem. The seat belt issue would legally bar recovery before a judge, but I can't go back to these poor people who've lost their only son with nothing but medical expenses. And you never know before a jury. They may ignore any contributory negligence claim.
Kepler: We're prepared for that.
Beach: And let me tell you something else. Your case isn't as strong as you think. You got a witness that no one's gonna believe.
Kepler: Who's that?
Beach: Rossini...the mechanic...the guy who missed the lug nuts?
Kepler: Rossini? I don't know what you hope to find there. His deposition is solidly on our side.

Beach: Yeah, but the deposition just doesn't ring true. I'm gonna give [him] a lot of trouble on cross-exam[ination]. I mean we're not gonna give up everything just to avoid a showdown in court! I can tell you that right now!

This is a classic example of how lawyers use law and facts in playing-out negotiations. They try to convince their opponents, or themselves, how the facts in their case will come out and how the law will be applied (or not applied) once they are in court. Lawyers negotiate by reference to what the court is likely to decide, based on the applicable law and the facts at hand. This type of negotiation is called *principled negotiation* because it is based on objective criteria, that is objective standards of fairness, or given certain facts and law, what the court is likely to decide.[20] Beach and Kepler were using principled negotiation techniques, negotiating on the basis of how the law and facts would appear in court.

But people using principled negotiation are at a serious disadvantage if they do not know what the correct standards of fairness are because they are unprepared on law or facts. Beach was dismally unprepared on both. He did not know about the new statute dealing with contributory negligence and he was too lazy or penny-pinching to do any further investigation in relation to Rossini. Consequently, he had low expectations of what he could achieve for his client in court. He was reduced to making empty threats. When Beach threatened a "showdown in court", Kepler could not take him seriously. Beach soon settled for a pathetic $2,500, nowhere near the $20,000 Kepler was authorised to pay.

With better preparation Beach would not have had such a low-value perception of his case. If he had researched the latest changes in the law of contributory negligence, he would not have conceded the seat belt issue. If he had followed his investigator's advice and instructed him to question Rossini further, he could at least have prepared some pointed questions for Kepler about the facts. For example, when Kepler, in answer to Beach's accusation about the mechanic, replied that his deposition was solidly on their side, Beach might have countered with: "To your knowledge, has Mr Rossini changed his evidence since that deposition?" Kepler would most certainly have given an evasive answer, but that would not have mattered since the reason for the question would be to create discomfort for Kepler and, hopefully, lower *his* expectations.

The Beach/Kepler dialogue demonstrates not only how principled negotiation works, but also that playing-out negotiation is a skill firmly rooted in the first two stages of playing out conflict — *defining legal wrongs* and *investigating the facts*. Lawyers need to build their cases

carefully on law and facts in those stages as well as prepare thoroughly
before they go into negotiations. This case-building and preparation can
also substantially narrow the gap between experience and inexperience.
For people not long out of law school who are intimidated by the
prospect of having to negotiate with experienced lawyers such as
Kepler, the problem they face is how to hold their own and protect
themselves from their own inexperience. *Knowing the law* and *knowing
the facts* increases the likelihood of solving their client's problem
satisfactorily. With a thoroughly researched view of what the case is
worth, a lawyer is more likely to have the confidence to settle on
appropriate terms, as well as to know when an offer is so out of line that
trial is the only alternative.

4. ADVOCACY

Like negotiation, advocacy builds on the earlier stages of the playing-out
conflict process and the ways in which the lawyer puts facts and law
together. Putting together facts and law in order to persuade the court is a
creative and often arduous process of theory, or story, development. And
as we have seen in Chapter 2, the theory of a case is a story designed to
persuade logically and emotionally (see Figure 2-5).

But what does the advocate do to ensure that the story is going to be
persuasive? Advocacy, the most complex of legal skills requires a
strategic, problem-solving approach to persuasion. Unlike negotiation,
in which a thorough grasp of facts and law can probably protect a new
lawyer from disaster, in advocacy, lawyers cannot just get by with facts
and law or basic skills and knowledge. In advocacy, just getting by is
equal to losing and advocacy is all about winning.

What factors are most important in this problem-solving approach to
advocacy? Two stand above the rest: understanding the advocate's role
and planning the case.

Understanding the advocate's role

Persuasion in the courtroom begins with lawyers understanding their
role as advocates clearly and how that role relates to the role and
authority of the judge. Inexperienced lawyers often have difficulty
developing an appropriate relationship with judges in the courtroom.
Because law school focuses on case law, it promotes the idea that judges
are the only repository of legal wisdom. This distorts students'
understanding of the legal system, what lawyers do, and their understanding of what judges do. This has a noticeable effect on their
relationship with judges when they first begin to learn courtroom skills.

In simulated advocacy exercises, I have seen many students fearful or distrustful of judges, perceiving them as remote, authority figures whose sole purpose in life is to expose the inadequacies of lawyers and demonstrate their own infallibility. It takes time for students to learn how to deal comfortably with judges and to understand that questions or comments from the bench are usually intended to clarify and test arguments, not to antagonise them or strike fear into their hearts.

Students have to learn that the advocate's role is one of problem-solver, not supplicant to a higher authority. Judges ordinarily *want* to be persuaded; to be persuaded is their job. Their job is not to oppress advocates. The advocate's job is to help judges reach a favourable decision, not to outsmart authority. To be helpful, advocates must realise that the judge, who usually plays a passive role, needs to be helped by counsel. Advocates need to plan their evidence and argument to advance their theory of the case so that the judge clearly understands it. The judge also needs to be guided in overcoming the factual and legal obstacles that stand in the way of being persuaded.

Facts and law are again at the forefront of what lawyers do, because judges need to feel logically and emotionally comfortable with the advocate's rendering of both. Advocates must try to see things from the judge's point of view, helping them make decisions that sit well with their minds and hearts. To achieve this, they need to see judges as human beings with a system of beliefs about people and society.[21] It can be counter-productive to make an argument on the basis of a principle that the judge is unlikely to believe in, *e.g.* young offenders are not responsible for the crimes they commit because they are victims of their environment or the police beat confessions out of every accused.[22] On the other hand, it is still the advocate's job to help judges make decisions that may run against their beliefs without challenging their whole system.

Judges, particularly magistrates, usually believe what police witnesses say because they can see that law enforcement personnel have a difficult and dangerous job. If judges are asked to decide in a way that contradicts police evidence, the defence advocate should present the case in such a way that the judge's fundamental belief in law enforcement is not challenged. An effective defence advocate may choose not to assert that the police have lied under oath, but instead try to paint a picture in ways that suggest the police had made a mistake, or that one of them was a rotten apple. In this way, most judges can acquit comfortably without feeling they have undermined the authority of the police.[23]

In persuading effectively, the advocate's appeal to the logical and emotional needs of the judge will not be enough if the advocate neglects ethical appeal. "Ethical appeal" refers not so much to the content of what the advocate says but to how the advocate is perceived by the judge.[24] Advocates who make an effective ethical appeal are those who leave the judge with the impression that they have good sense, moral character and goodwill toward others.[25] This is why the advocate's reputation for ethical conduct has such an impact on the relationship between advocate and judge. Being aware of the impact of ethical, emotional and logical appeals to the judge probably represents the highest level of awareness in understanding that relationship.

Planning the case

Once advocates understand their relationship to the court, they are better able to develop a theory, or story, that is likely to be persuasive. This is a complex process that can best be accomplished with strategic planning and painstaking preparation. It is like planning for war. As in war, half-measures are as pointless as inconclusive outcomes, so the advocate's mind and resources must be completely focused on the goal to be achieved. Like most experienced advocates, Sir David Napley views the conduct of trial as war. He takes a problem-solving approach to trial planning viewing it as akin to planning for a military operation.[26]

An effective trial plan should include the following procedure:

1. identifying the goal to be achieved (*i.e.* what the theory is and how to prove it);
2. identifying the factors affecting the achievement of the goal (*i.e.* who the available witnesses are, what the evidence will be and how to prove the facts);
3. analysing the options (*i.e.* what strategies and tactics are available); and
4. designing the plan (*i.e.* what steps are needed to carry out the chosen option).[27]

To plan the case effectively in this way requires thoughtful and thorough preparation. This is true, for example, in planning cross-examination. In Rumpole's shoplifting case, his theory was that his client forgot to pay for the goods because the shop assistant was too preoccupied with chatting to take his money. To prove the theory, he used tactics in cross-examining the store detective that were designed to show inattentive shop assistants were responsible for his client forgetting to pay — not his client.

Cross-examination is a particularly delicate area, because asking the wrong question can easily undermine one's theory of the case. In a similar shoplifting case, described by Napley, the accused was a foreigner who while shopping in the store, ran out of local currency. Her defence — Napley's theory of the case — was that she left the store to go across the street to Barclay's Bank so she could change some dollars into sterling and return to pay for the goods. She was stopped by the store detective outside the store before she could get to the bank. After the store detective called in the police, the accused told them she was on her way to the bank to exchange money.

Napley described how to plan and prepare both cross-examination of the store detective as well as the introduction of other evidence. A direct approach to cross-examine the store detective was risky. If he suggested to the detective directly that the accused was heading toward the bank at the time she was stopped, the detective could give an unwanted answer such as: "No, she was going the other way".[28]

As with much cross-examination, an indirect approach was much safer. His strategy would be to try to get the detective indirectly to corroborate his theory of the case. First he would secure a witness from Barclay's Bank to testify his client had exchanged money there on previous occasions. As a witness for the defence, this bank employee would testify after the store detective. Napley would cross-examine the store detective by asking step-by-step questions to lay a foundation. For example, Napley would ask if there was in fact a Barclay's Bank across the street, and if the detective heard the accused say to the police she was going there to change money. In this case, the store detective had to answer yes to both questions. Napley would ask the detective whether the detective had checked at the bank to see if the accused was known there. The detective would most probably answer no. Having elicited these answers, he would then have a solid foundation for the evidence to be given both by the bank employee and the accused, and for his closing argument later on.[29]

This, of course, is only one small aspect of strategic planning, but it reveals how critical each small part of the strategic plan is to the whole and to how the story is going to be told. In addition, each small part of the plan may involve a great deal of work and skill. For example, approaching bank employees, questioning them and inducing one or more to testify is likely to be a difficult job. Napley's comments on trial planning highlight what may be the key to competent advocacy. The competent, or perhaps excellent, advocate not only has a persuasive story to tell, but a thoroughly-prepared, highly-detailed, strategic plan for telling it.[30]

MANAGING UNCERTAINTY: BUILDING THE CASE

The playing-out conflict process can be viewed as a progression toward
the goal of winning or settling by building the case with facts and law.
The effectiveness of negotiation depends to a considerable degree on
how well the lawyer has developed, and then grasped, facts and law. The
effectiveness of advocacy depends to a considerable degree on strategic
planning — how carefully and creatively the lawyer builds the theory of
the case and how he or she puts together facts and law to support it.

No matter how much strategic planning and thinking conflict players
do, however, they cannot control outcomes completely. No one can
control the outcome of a trial and no one can safely predict it either. No
one can say a negotiated or mediated settlement will produce a better
result than a trial. The process of playing out conflict to win or reach a
peaceful resolution is ruled by constant uncertainty until the goal is
achieved or lost.

Effectively managing the problem-solving process at the point of
deciding to continue fighting or to settle is the defining moment of the
playing-out conflict situation because it is at this point that the
uncertainty is brought on to centre stage. If the client settles, he or she is
uncertain whether the settlement is better than going to trial. If the client
decides to go to trial, he or she is uncertain whether that decision will
bring triumph or defeat. Binder and Price say that the ultimate decision
should rest with the client, based on the option that would give the client
the most satisfaction.[31]

But this, in turn, requires knowledge of the client's personality. If, for
example, one client is more of a risk-taker than another, though they may
have exactly the same case, the risk-taker may decide to go to trial while
the other client does not.[32] It is the lawyer's job to manage this
decision-making process, which requires skill, confidence and patience.

In 1973, in a New York City court, a 21-year-old student named Gail
Kalmowitz sued some doctors for malpractice. Ms Kalmowitz claimed
the doctors had caused her near blindness by administering "uncon-
trolled amounts of oxygen" to her after she had been born prematurely.
Her right eye was removed at age six and her vision in her left eye was so
limited she had to use a cane and read Braille. Ms Kalmowitz sued the
doctors for $2 million, and an offer from the doctors to settle for
$165,000 was made but had not been accepted. After the closing
arguments, the jury started deliberations and then quickly sent word to
the judge that it had reached a verdict and wanted to return to court.

At this point, Ms Kalmowitz panicked, thinking that the jury's quick
decision meant she had lost the case. Before the jury could return, she
accepted the out-of-court settlement offer of $165,000. Afterward, Ms

Managing uncertainty: building a case

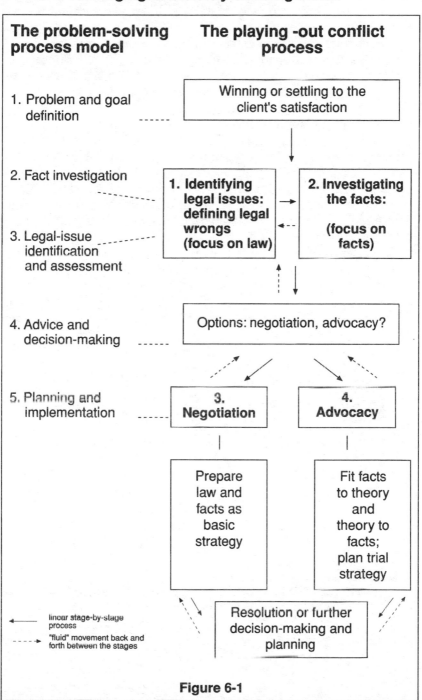

The problem-solving process model	The playing -out conflict process
1. Problem and goal definition	Winning or settling to the client's satisfaction
2. Fact investigation	1. Identifying legal issues: defining legal wrongs (focus on law) → 2. Investigating the facts: (focus on facts)
3. Legal-issue identification and assessment	
4. Advice and decision-making	Options: negotiation, advocacy?
5. Planning and implementation	3. Negotiation — 4. Advocacy
	Prepare law and facts as basic strategy — Fit facts to theory and theory to facts; plan trial strategy
	Resolution or further decision-making and planning

← linear stage-by-stage process

--→ "fluid" movement back and forth between the stages

Figure 6-1

Kalmowitz found out the jury had awarded her $900,000. It was, however, too late as the judge had made the agreement binding as an out-of-court settlement.[33]

The chapter closes with this anecdote because the decision Ms Kalmowitz took was opposite to the decision taken by O.J. Simpson and Rex Carr's clients discussed at the beginning of Chapter 5. They chose to go to trial and let the court decide. Ms Kalmowitz chose to settle before the court decided. Her fateful decision shows how uncertain and unpredictable the conflict-playing process is even when a case is settled.

This should not lead people to think, however, that the lawyer's job of trying to manage uncertainty is a futile exercise. After all, without all the hard work done by Ms Kalmowitz's attorneys, she might never have managed to elicit any offer at all, let alone one for $165,000 (in 1973 dollars). Ms Kalmowitz, having undergone terrible suffering wanted justice and her attorneys transformed the uncertainty of getting it into the certainty of a concrete offer of money.

Competent conflict players do know how to manage uncertainty throughout the problem-solving process. By defining legal wrongs, investigating facts, negotiating with a firm grasp of law and facts and carefully planning trial strategy, lawyers can manage uncertainty by improving the odds, building their case at every stage and instilling confidence in their clients.

---

[1] A.K.A. Kiralfy, *The English Legal System* (Sweet & Maxwell, London, 8th ed., 1990), pp.29–32.
[2] [1893] Q.B. 256.
[3] A.W.B. Simpson, "Quackery and Contract Law: The Case of the Carbolic Smoke Ball", (1985) XIV *Journal of Legal Studies*, 345 at 378.
[4] *ibid.*
[5] [1932] A.C. 562.
[6] K.M. Stanton, *The Modern Law of Tort* (Sweet & Maxwell, London, 1994), pp.29–30.
[7] Cecil A. Wright, Allen M. Linden, Lewis N. Klar, *Canadian Tort Law: Cases, Notes & Materials* (Butterworths, Toronto & Vancouver, 9th ed., 1990), pp.8.3–8.4.
[8] Martin R. Taylor, "Mrs Donoghue's Journey" in *Donoghue v. Stevenson and the Modern Law of Negligence: the Paisley Papers, The Proceedings of the Paisley Conference on the Law of Negligence* (eds Peter T. Burns and Susan J. Lyons) (Continuing Legal Education Society of B.C., Vancouver, 1991), pp.1–8.
[9] *Donoghue v. Stevenson* [1932] A.C. 562 at 564.
[10] Martin R. Taylor, *op.cit.* p.6.
[11] William W. McBryde, "The Story of the Snail in the Bottle Case", *The Proceedings of the Paisley Conference on the Law of Negligence, op.cit.*, p.43.
[12] *ibid.* p.44
[13] *ibid.*

[14] See David Binder and David Bergman, *Fact Investigation: From Hypothesis To Proof* (West Publishing Co., St. Paul, Minn., 1984), pp.2–8.

[15] *ibid.*, pp.240–243.

[16] See e.g., David A. Binder, Susan C. Price, *Legal Interviewing and Counselling: A Client-Centred Approach*, (West Publishing Co., St. Paul, Minn., 1977), pp.32–33.

[17] Paul Brodeur, "Annals of Law, The Asbestos Industry on Trial", *The New Yorker* (The New York Magazine, New York) June 17, 1985, 45–111 at 68–70.

[18] American Bar Association, *Legal Ethics: Applying the Model Rules, Discussion Guides for the ABA Videolaw Seminar* (American Bar Association, 1984), pp.61–67.

[19] Gary Bellow and Bea Moulton, *The Lawyering Process: Negotiation* (Foundation Press, Mineola, New York, 1981), p. 253.

[20] See generally, Roger Fisher and William Ury, *Getting To Yes: Negotiating Agreement Without Giving In* (Penguin Books, Middlesex, 1983), Chap. 5.

[21] Jeffrey Hartje and Mark Wilson, *Lawyers Work: Counselling, Problem Solving, Advocacy and The Conduct of Litigation* (Butterworth Legal Publishers, Seattle, 1984), pp.307–310.

[22] *ibid.*

[23] Keith Evans, *Advocacy At The Bar: A Beginner's Guide* (Financial Training Publications, London, 1983), pp.82–83.

[24] Hartje and Wison, *op.cit.*, p.311.

[25] *ibid.*

[26] Sir David Napley, *The Technique of Persuasion* (Sweet & Maxwell, London, 1991), p.74

[27] *ibid.*, p.75.

[28] *ibid.*, p.81.

[29] *ibid.*, pp.81–82.

[30] The idea that strategic planning may be the cornerstone of excellence in advocacy was provided to the author by Tony Tobin who has conducted comprehensive (as yet unpublished) research into the subject in Ontario.

[31] David A. Binder, Susan C. Price, *op. cit.*, p.148.

[32] *ibid.*, pp.149–150.

[33] Karen Oliver, "Blind Student Settles Suit—A Moment Too Soon", *The Boston Globe*, March 23, 1973, cited in Gary Bellow and Bea Moulton, *op cit.*, pp.158–159.

CHAPTER 7

CONFLICT BLOCKING: THEORY AND PRACTICE

Like Geoffrey Chaucer writing six centuries ago in *The Canterbury Tales*, many people today still see conflict-blockers as professional sorcerers who exercise magical powers to relieve clients of their money at opportune moments. In the Kurt Vonnegut novel, *God Bless You Mr Rosewater*,[1] a law student is told by his professor the way to get ahead:

"... a lawyer should be looking for situations where large amounts of money are about to change hands. ... In every big transaction, there is a magic moment during which a man has surrendered a treasure, and during which the man who is due to receive it has not yet done so. An alert lawyer will make that moment his own, possessing the treasure for a magic microsecond, taking a little of it, passing it on. If the man who is to receive the treasure is unused to wealth, has an inferiority complex and shapeless feelings of guilt, as most people do, the lawyer can often take as much as half the bundle, and still receive the recipient's blubbering thanks."[2]

Fiction aside, the work of the conflict blocker is neither larcenous or opportunistic, but based on real social and economic needs. Nevertheless, Vonnegut's satire does contain a hint of truth: conflict blockers frequently make their living by acting for clients when assets change hands. But in these situations blockers do not perform sleight of hand, they aggressively protect their clients' assets and interests.

In this respect, blocking conflicts is similar to playing out conflict. Both involve aggressive advocacy on behalf of clients. Commercial transactions provide the best examples of how this advocacy works because they are common in law practice and because the transfer of money and property is accompanied by risks that the specialised skills of conflict blockers can address.

THE CONFLICT BETWEEN DEBTORS AND CREDITORS

The ancient conflict between creditors and debtors provides a revealing and easy-to-understand context for what the commercial blocker does: since creditors have always wanted to lend with as much security as possible and debtors to borrow with as little security as possible, the potential for conflict between the two is high. Lawyers for creditors have always worked at solving the problem of how to strengthen their security, and lawyers for debtors have tried to minimise their liability.

Creditors' lawyers use blocking tactics to strengthen their security. Even in simple loan agreements, security can be strengthened by inducing the borrower to pay by discouraging default. One of the most common of these tactics is the *balloon payment* or *acceleration* clause in a loan agreement with scheduled payments. A form of it reads as follows:

> In default of any scheduled payment, the whole amount of principal and interest then outstanding shall become due and payable and the borrower shall forthwith pay the same to the lender.

A simple clause such as this achieves a great deal for the lender because, without it, if the borrower goes into default on one or more of the payments, and the payment schedule has not yet come to an end, the lender would only be entitled to sue the borrower for the arrears and not for the total amount outstanding. The *balloon payment* clause provides a disincentive for the borrower to default: if the borrower defaults, he or she must immediately pay the entire amount — "the ballooned" or "accelerated" amount — outstanding.

In this case, blocking action serves both as a preventive and pre-emptive measure. It prevents the conflict that arises from default but, even if that conflict should occur, it pre-empts defences by the borrower. If the lender sues for repayment of the debt, the borrower cannot defend by saying, I owe only the payments I have defaulted on, not the entire amount I have borrowed. This strengthens the lender's case if and when the playing-out process gets underway. Used in this way, conflict blocking is a form of tactical advocacy.

A SEESAW BATTLE BETWEEN DEBTORS AND CREDITORS

Limited liability

Although creditors typically have more bargaining power than debtors, debtors are not without creative legal resources to protect their interests. Before the invention of the limited liability company, investors in business ventures could be deemed partners and be liable as debtors for vast amounts of money in the conduct of the business in which they invested. The invention of the limited liability company was an important solution to investors'/debtors' problems in that it enabled

large amounts of capital to be raised from investors without subjecting
them to claims beyond the limit of their investment. Investors were
transformed into shareholders. This provided an incentive for people to
launch substantial business ventures because, as shareholders, they had
limited downside risk but unlimited potential profit.

Guarantees

For many small companies today, however, the protection that limited
liability affords is illusory. When small companies borrow money from
banks to finance operations, limited liability does not, in practice, spare
shareholders when bank loans go into default. This is because, in small
companies, directors and shareholders are usually the same people, and
banks circumvent limited liability by requiring these directors to sign
unlimited guarantees of loans made by the bank to the company. Limited
liability is an ingenious solution to raising capital and limiting risk, but
the standard bank guarantee is an ingenious counter-solution for banks
that require security for their loans.

Debtors' defences to guarantees

The courts, however, are highly protective of guarantors' rights. Banks
have chased countless numbers of guarantors to honour the debts of
principal debtors, and guarantors' lawyers have come up with numerous
inventive defences to the banks' claims. The courts, in their wisdom,
have seen the merits of many of these defences. Legal scholars have
suggested various reasons for this tendency, but the underlying reason is
sympathy for guarantors. Courts often feel sympathetic towards
guarantors when the bank's dealings with the principal debtor prejudices
the guarantor's position or when guarantors' business plans go awry or
when the bank is perceived to have lent money irresponsibly. This
sympathy seems to have encouraged conflict players to produce many
clever, highly-technical, defences for guarantors.

  This is where conflict blockers and their powerful advocacy enter the
scene. With conflict players continuing to find ways to free their
guarantor clients from the shackles of the guarantee, blockers continue
to find ways to fasten them on. The decision of *Coutts and Co. v.
Browne-Lecky and Others*[3] and its aftermath illustrate the point. In
Coutts, a minor was the principal debtor but the guarantors were adults.
When Coutts sued the guarantors, their lawyer's argument was that since
the debt, incurred by an underage person, was void, so should the
guarantee that covered it be void. The bank argued, however, that a

specific clause in the guarantee effectively blocked that defence. Part of that clause said:

> ...... this guarantee ......shall not in any way be prejudiced or affected by the want of borrowing powers on the part of the debtor...... or of the directors or managers or officials of the debtor or by any excess in the exercise of such powers (if any)...... or by the fact that there is no principal debtor primarily liable......"

This clause, the bank's lawyers said, preserved the effect of the guarantee even in the event the principal debtor's liability was void. For example, if the principal debtor was a company and it turned out that it had no constitutional powers to borrow, the clause still preserved the guarantee. Furthermore, went the bank's argument, even if there was "no principal debtor primarily liable" the guarantor would still be liable.

At first glance, this seems like a strong argument. After all, the clause did say that the guarantee, "shall not in any way be prejudiced or affected...by the fact that there is no principal debtor primarily liable...". But the guarantors' side had an even better argument: a minor could not be a "principal debtor" because a minor was legally incapable of incurring a debt. *By implication*, the clause therefore excluded minors. As the court said:

> "every time the word 'debtor' is used ... this infant who, by statute, is incapable of incurring a debt of this kind, appears to me to be *impliedly* excluded. The whole structure of that clause, as I interpret it, is inapplicable to an individual in any case; it is quite plainly drawn with meticulous care... to cover cases where companies have borrowed money *ultra vires*, [*i.e.* without proper authority] and so on."

The clause was obviously meant to refer to companies not to children, so the court ruled in favour of the guarantors. Of course, other reasons stood behind the ruling such as the rule of interpretation that a document should be construed against the party (the bank) that drafted it, but the court's natural sympathy for guarantors undoubtedly influenced its hairsplitting interpretation.

Creditors' blocking tactics

Interpretation favouring guarantors is constantly sending the banks' lawyers back to their drawing boards. After *Coutts*, for instance, the banking lawyers again went to work to make sure that the issue raised in that case was never raised again in a court of law. They redrafted their guarantees in the hope of blocking that particular issue forever. They came up with a variety of solutions such as this one, found in a standard-form bank guarantee:

"All sums of money which may not be recoverable from the Guarantor on the footing of a guarantee by reason of any legal limitation disability or incapacity on or of the Principal shall nevertheless be recoverable from the Guarantor as sole principal debtor."

This post-*Coutts* clause should be an effective blocking solution to the problem. The clause means that if the principal debtor is underage (*i.e.* under a "legal disability"), guarantors are no longer guarantors; they are instantly deemed "principal debtors", and are liable to pay as such.

Another example of the many ways banking lawyers have responded to defences devised by guarantors' lawyers relates to the defence of *prejudice*. Whenever the guarantor could prove that the lender had in some way varied the terms of the loan to the principal debtor, such as granting more time to pay, or releasing existing security without obtaining the express consent of the guarantor, the guarantor was seen to be prejudiced by this variation. A rule developed that this prejudice was alone sufficient to release the guarantor from liability.[4]

This rule caused conflict-blocking lawyers to come up with counter measures for their banking clients. They devised both drafting and procedural solutions. The drafting solution was to insert new clauses into guarantees, one of which is as follows:

"You (the Guarantor) shall be at liberty without thereby affecting your rights against the Guarantor at any time to determine enlarge or vary any credit to the Principal to vary exchange abstain from perfecting or release any other securities held or to be held by you for or on account of the monies intended to be hereby secured or any part thereof to renew bills and promissory notes in any manner and to compound with give time for payment to accept compositions from and make any other arrangements with the Principal or any obligants on bills notes or other securities held or to be held by you for or on behalf of the Principal."

This provision, known as a *time and indulgence* clause,[5] blocks guarantors from later claiming that granting time and indulgence to the principal debtor prejudices them. But then the banking lawyers also devised a procedural solution: they advised their banking clients not to rely on this clause alone to pre-empt the defence of prejudice. Play it safe, they told their clients, change your procedures. Whenever a variation of the underlying loan is contemplated, guarantors should be informed immediately and their written consent to the variation should be requested.[6] This became a fail-safe blocking action. If the clause failed to do the job, the procedure of getting the guarantor's consent would probably succeed.

All competent conflict blockers (not just banking lawyers) use the law as a backdrop for drafting documents and designing procedures: they identify the legal issues and draft provisions or design procedures to block claims that might be made in relation to those issues. These lawyers practise preventive law since their aim is to prevent the client from getting into a conflict or outright litigation.[7] Conflicts are expensive and should be avoided whenever possible. In reality, however, effective blocking action does not mean conflict is necessarily avoided. Sometimes conflict occurs no matter how airtight the drafting or the procedures. When conflict does occur, prior effective action can *block* it, weakening or neutralising the other side's arguments, and reducing their leverage when the conflict is played out. In the case of a bank's claim against a guarantor, if both the principal debtor and guarantor do not pay, legal action is inevitable, but a well-drafted guarantee and pre-emptive procedures in dealing with the principal debtor will block the usual defences so that the bank's case will be strong and inexpensive to prosecute.

The floating charge

In relation to lending to companies, an even more ingenious form of security than the guarantee in English law is the *floating charge*. The development of the floating charge is a story of how lawyers solved a problem created by the law. The problem was, how could the assets of a company be secured — or *charged* — when so many of them were being bought and sold or were not yet even in existence? If the company owned land, the bank could always take a fixed charge (or a mortgage) against it, but if land was insufficient security or the company did not own any land, then what? Whoever bought products from the company in the ordinary course of business would not buy them if they were "charged". And no bank would want to lend without securing the company's existing and future assets, including its inventory. Under the common law these future assets could not be secured.

The solution was described by Roy Goode as "a further manifestation of the English genius for harnessing the most abstract conceptions to the service of commerce."[8] What the lawyers dreamed up was to draft a charge so that the security did not actually attach to the company's assets, but rather "floated" over the company's assets whether existing or after-acquired. The company could thus trade in its assets without interference, and the bank need not fear assets slipping from its grasp since those traded would be replaced by new ones.

When default occurred as defined under the charge, the creditor could *crystallise* it, in effect transforming it into a *fixed* charge, attaching it to all corporate assets to which it related. In practice, this meant the creditor could appoint a receiver, who would take over from the directors and have the authority to deal with all corporate assets.

The concept of securing after-acquired assets is not new. Under Roman law, the *hypotheca* could create a charge over a class of assets that was constantly changing.[9] Even so, until the middle of the nineteenth century, common-law judges had always rejected this concept. After-acquired assets could not be secured and when companies became insolvent, floating chargeholders would not gain priority over unsecured creditors. This created a problem for both lenders and borrowers: lenders would not want to lend without security, and borrowers would have difficulty finding willing lenders so they could carry on business. Driven by the needs of both parties, blockers solved the problem by creating the floating charge, and conflict players fought to defend the concept in the courts. In the latter part of the nineteenth century, they finally persuaded the courts of the viability of the concept using equitable principles to circumvent the common law.[10]

USING INTERNAL REMEDIES TO BLOCK CONFLICT

In situations where conflict blockers see that a conflict is likely to arise, they can devise inexpensive methods to block it. The floating charge is a good example of this type of preventive conflict blocking. If borrowers do not pay, lenders do not have to sue and then try to enforce judgment; they simply retain the services of a receiver to take possession of the assets. The creditor's remedy is found inside the transaction, not in the courtroom. It is therefore called an *internal remedy*.

Another, simpler, example of an internal remedy is the provision for payment and forfeiture of a deposit in the course of selling an asset. In the sale of an asset the seller's lawyer usually provides in the agreement for payment of a deposit and, in the event the buyer fails to complete the transaction, the seller forfeits the deposit as "liquidated damages". By including such a provision, the seller's lawyer induces the buyer to complete by jacking up his investment in the transaction; in the event the buyer does not complete the seller does not have to chase the buyer for damages. The seller can simply keep what has been paid as a deposit as a reasonable pre-estimate of the damages the seller has suffered.

A more complex example of an internal remedy is the *compulsory buy-out* in shareholders' agreements. Since shareholders in small companies frequently quarrel, it is particularly difficult to avoid conflict. A carefully drawn agreement that anticipates these quarrels can provide a mechanism for blocking them. One of them is called a *compulsory buy-out* or *shotgun* clause. This is a provision that solves the problem of what to do when shareholders, who work together in a small company, disagree with each other or are fed up with one another and no longer want to stay together in business.

Without an agreement to establish what they would do in the event of such a situation, one shareholder could apply to court to wind up the company, or bring suit against other shareholders citing prejudicial conduct.[11]

In a shareholders' agreement with two shareholders and compulsory buyout provisions, one party, "Oscar", can offer his shares for sale to the other party, "Bea", on certain terms. Bea then has two options — to buy Oscar's shares on those terms, or to sell her own shares to Oscar on those same terms. If she does nothing, she is deemed to have agreed to sell all her shares to Oscar on those terms. Some lawyers think that compulsory buyouts are unfair when one shareholder has considerably more financial clout than the other, making it virtually impossible for the less financially endowed to buy. When the parties are relatively equal, however, the compulsory buyout is an excellent method of blocking costly court proceedings.

Other types of more general internal remedies are used by lawyers to block conflict. For example, instead of trying to list every possible type of conflict and then provide a specific remedy for it, the lawyer can simply include a general dispute-resolution provision such as an arbitration clause, or a clause providing for a third party to settle a dispute if it arises. This has the advantage of simplicity. The disadvantage is that resolving the dispute through arbitration may be less costly than court proceedings but it may still result in substantial legal costs.

BLOCKING CONFLICTS IN A NON-COMPETITIVE SITUATION

Conflict-blocking does not always involve a competitive relationship between people entering into commercial agreements. It can also involve the creation of a trust or a will. In the creation of a trust, legal ownership of assets is transferred to a trustee in order to facilitate investment, avoid taxes or protect assets from creditors. The trust normally provides a degree of freedom of action for the trustee, while delineating the duties the trustee owes to the beneficial owner of the assets. A thoughtfully structured trust and well-drawn trust document will block potential conflict with taxation authorities and creditors, yet still enable the trustee to manage the trust efficiently.

Wills also provide many opportunities for conflict blocking. The following problem about a will described by a lawyer, illustrates the point:

The "Will" Problem

I have a client with quite a bit of money and not much to do. She comes into the office often to update her will. She is a widow with three daughters, two of whom are married with children. The unmarried, youngest one is a big disappointment to her mother. She has a history of minor psychiatric problems but refuses to get psychiatric counselling at the university where she is a student.

The last time my client wanted a will updated, her instructions were to cut the youngest daughter out of the will completely. I asked her why she wanted to do this. We had a long discussion and she explained in detail what a disappointment her youngest child was, how she was unwilling to help herself and take responsibility for her life.

I advised her against disinheriting her. I explained that when someone who has a will dies, and a child feels unhappy about the provisions, she can apply to court for a will variation. The court has a discretion to give her something from the estate. So I told her to provide a small amount in the will for that daughter and prepare a letter to me explaining her reasons for providing that amount. If her letter showed good judgment and the amount provided was large enough, the daughter would be less likely to sue later on.

I also told her that if she cut the daughter out completely, she risked having the estate eaten up by legal costs in the event of a contested claim being made, to say nothing of the animosity that would be created between the sisters.

Alternatively, I said, she could distribute *inter vivos* gifts to the children now (*i.e.* gifts while she was alive) or set up a trust with them as beneficiaries. I also suggested she see a counsellor to see if she could improve her relationship with the daughter. But she did not like any of my suggestions. She wanted to punish her daughter. She told me, "You're missing the point! I want her to *know* she's being left out!

The money will do more harm than good. If she knows the money is coming, she won't do anything to help herself."

It was at this point that a light bulb went on over my head. I said: "You want her to know you feel like cutting her out, right? Well then write her a letter telling her that and the reasons why. If it's satisfaction you want you'll have plenty of it because you'll be able to see her reaction while you're still *alive*. Then you let me do your will and include provisions for her in it. After you're gone, that will probably give her such a pleasant surprise, she won't bring action against the estate. The estate will be saved thousands in legal costs."

To my relief, my client liked the idea. Her maternal instinct to try to help her daughter overrode her desire to teach her a lesson.

So we went ahead with it. She wrote a letter to her daughter that I had to amend before it went out. It was too angry and direct. Of course, it was what one might expect an angry mother to write. But it could be misconstrued by a third party such as a judge. So I softened the language, transforming accusations into reasoned protests. In the letter, mum was able to express her hurt and disappointment and ask the daughter to pull up her boot straps. Mum also mentioned the inheritance and her fear that it would be squandered in an irresponsible way by the daughter.

We then discussed how to benefit the daughter in the will. After some discussion, I was able to get her to agree to provide quite generously for the daughter, although not nearly as generously as for the other two daughters. The provision for the youngest daughter was subject to a corporate managed trust with strict conditions. The other two daughters were to receive their interests in the estate with no conditions. I drafted the will and she executed it.

Most wills are drafted with the purpose of preventing conflict among the survivors. In this case, if the client had been allowed to carry out her initial wishes, she would have probably created much conflict among her children. The lawyer did her job by pointing out the potential problems and persuading the client to get back on the conflict-blocking track.

The lawyer viewed her advocacy as protecting the client from herself, protecting the estate from the ravages of legal conflict, and preventing the will itself from being litigated. If that were to occur, the lawyer's judgment and competence would be called into question. If the matter were to end up in court, the lawyer would have to endure the embarrassment of cross-examination and perhaps criticism by the court. No lawyer wants a transaction she has designed or a document she has drafted to be under the litigation spotlight. An important feature of solving conflict-blocking problems is that the lawyer is as motivated as the client to ensure the risk of conflict is minimised. The conflict-blocking lawyer has to protect the client's rights as well as to preserve her own reputation.

USING THE PROBLEM-SOLVING PROCESS MODEL TO BLOCK CONFLICTS

What would the Will Scenario look like if it were broken up into the stages of the process model?

1. Problem and goal definition

The client's initial goal was to do a new will and disinherit her daughter. That goal defined the problem for the lawyer: how could she draft a will unlikely to be contested, but one that would follow the client's wishes?

2. Fact investigation

The lawyer wanted to know why the client wanted to disinherit her daughter. The lawyer's questioning was guided by issues in the law of variation of wills. Under this law, dependants can claim that the deceased failed to make adequate provision for them in the will. The daughter, if still a student, could apply to court for an order against the estate.[12]

3. Legal-issue identification and assessment

Having gathered and evaluated the facts, the lawyer concluded that a decision to disinherit the youngest daughter would raise an issue related to variation of the will. She felt that such a decision could incite litigation. She made a prediction assessment that the daughter would be able to maintain a credible position on an application to court to vary the will.

4. Advice and decision-making

Based on the facts and law, the lawyer concluded that blocking the potential conflict among the daughters should be the client's main goal. One solution, she suggested, was to give the youngest daughter something and to leave a written record of the reason. Another was to distribute part of the estate *inter vivos* so that there would be fewer assets to fight about after the mother's death.

The client rejected both of these options. The lawyer, in a flash of inspiration (the light bulb went on) redefined the problem, taking it back to Stage 1. The problem was no longer how to draft the will to achieve the client's disinheritance goal without provoking conflict. The real problem for the client was how to control her daughter in a way that would expose the estate to a lower risk of conflict. The way to do this was to exercise control through a written communication separate from the will — that is, through the client's letter to the daughter. In any subsequent legal conflict, this letter could be used as evidence of the client's intention. But viewed against the actual provisions of the will, which were to provide for the youngest daughter, the client's conduct would appear so reasonable as likely to block that daughter from pursuing her claim. The client agreed to this solution.

5. Planning and implementation

The lawyer finessed the problem by splitting the solution into two plans, each implemented separately — one in the form of a letter, the other in the form of a will. The lawyer carefully planned both, even helping to write the letter to soften it. She struck a balance between permitting her client to vent her feelings and using measured language so as not to provoke the daughter into suing. She also made sure that if the daughter did sue, the letter would make the client's decision-making look reasonable and prudent in the event it was later called into question.

LINEARITY, FLEXIBILITY AND DEVELOPING PLANS

Compared to playing-out conflict situations, conflict-blocking situations usually have clearer and more finite goals with a limited time horizon. Because of this, lawyers can develop linear, step-by-step plans to deal with them. Standard documents and procedures, or *plans*, are applicable to many conflict-blocking transactions. For example, when lawyers draft wills, they do not think up new clauses for each client. They can select different sets of standard clauses to meet their clients' goals. They can also modify clauses, or create new ones, to comply with more specific instructions.

It appears that well-designed plans often have similar structures, even when they are developed in different common-law jurisdictions. An English will, guarantee, corporate acquisition or property conveyance shares many of the same features as corresponding Canadian, Australian, Hong Kong or American transactions. The structures, steps and documents have been developed through the collective practice of lawyers whose expertise has been brought to bear on the host of problems these transactions present. It seems that because human

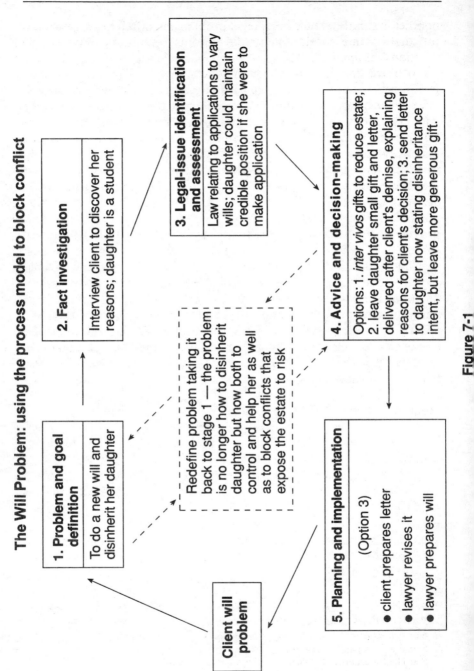

The Will Problem: using the process model to block conflict

1. Problem and goal definition

To do a new will and disinherit her daughter

2. Fact investigation

Interview client to discover her reasons; daughter is a student

3. Legal-issue identification and assessment

Law relating to applications to vary wills; daughter could maintain credible position if she were to make application

Redefine problem taking it back to stage 1 — the problem is no longer how to disinherit daughter but how both to control and help her as well as to block conflicts that expose the estate to risk

4. Advice and decision-making

Options: 1. *inter vivos* gifts to reduce estate; 2. leave daughter small gift and letter, delivered after client's demise, explaining reasons for client's decision; 3. send letter to daughter now stating disinheritance intent, but leave more generous gift.

5. Planning and implementation

(Option 3)
● client prepares letter
● lawyer revises it
● lawyer prepares will

Client will problem

Figure 7-1

conflict is similar everywhere, legal problems in different common-law jurisdictions are similar and so lawyers have come up with similar solutions for them.

To block conflicts for clients, lawyers have to know the standard documents required to complete a transaction. In addition, they have to know the standard procedural steps, the legal significance of each step and how they all fit together. Because conflict-blocking solutions involve so much in the way of both documents and procedures (*i.e.* plans) lawyers need to know and understand them as well as the context in which they operate. *Knowing the plans* means understanding how they were developed in the first place as solutions to old problems. A lawyer given the task of redrafting a guarantee for a bank client should not modify a post-*Coutts* provision without understanding how that provision was developed and what it means. Only with this historical perspective, do lawyers have a solid foundation on which to develop plans that deal effectively with new problems.

But knowing the plans is just a prerequisite to competent conflict-blocking, it is not equal to it. As was revealed in the (relatively simple) will problem, the process of problem solving requires both *linear* and *flexible* approaches. The lawyer's linear approach took her through the stages and prompted her to use standard procedures and documents in drafting the will. But the problem was ultimately solved when she used a flexible approach, retracing steps, taking a second look at the problem and developing a new plan to meet the client's redefined goals (see Figure 7-1, opposite).

[1] K. Vonnegut, *"God Bless You Mr Rosewater"*, (Dell, New York, 1970) cited in Ronald J. Gilson, "Value Creation By Business Lawyers: Legal Skills and Asset Pricing", (1984) 94 *Yale Law Journal*, 239–313 at 241.

[2] Vonnegut, *ibid.*, p.9.

[3] [1946] 2 All E.R. 207.

[4] *Yates v. Evans* (1892) 61 L.J.Q.B. 446.

[5] P.J.M. Fidler, *Sheldon and Fidler's Practice and Law of Banking* (MacDonald and Evans, London, 11th ed., 1982), pp.326, 723.

[6] *ibid.*, p.326.

[7] Robert C. Dick, *Legal Drafting* (Carswell, Toronto, 2nd ed., 1985), p.1.

[8] R. Goode, *Commercial Law* (Penguin Books, London, 2nd ed., 1995), p.731.

[9] Robert R. Pennington, "The Genesis of The Floating Charge", (1960) 23 *Modern Law Review*, 630–646, at 634.

[10] See, *e.g.*, *Holroyd v. Marshall* (1862) 10 H.L. Cas. 191.

[11] See, *e.g.* Companies Act 1985, s. 459(1).

[12] See The Inheritance (Provision For Family and Dependants) Act 1975.

CHAPTER 8

THE CONFLICT BLOCKING PROCESS

Chapter 7 considered conflict blocking as primarily concerned with the creation of documents. This chapter considers conflict blocking from a broader transactional perspective, looking at how the whole design of, and process of carrying out, commercial transactions promotes conflict-blocking goals. The chapter is organised into four topics:

1. the executory contract;
2. blocking conflicts in negotiation;
3. the blocking endgame; and
4. blocking and competence.

1. THE EXECUTORY CONTRACT

When people buy an expensive asset such as property or a business, they need time to investigate the asset to ascertain its value. At the same time, they do not want the asset to be sold while they are investigating. In transactions of this type lawyers have developed a mechanism that gives them the time and opportunity to protect their clients' interests, as well as to investigate and block potential conflicts before arranging for transfer of ownership. This mechanism is called the executory contract.

In a typical executory contract, a buyer agrees to buy and a seller agrees to sell something, but they also agree to transfer ownership — to close or complete the agreement — at a later, specified date. After the agreement is signed, but before the specified date, the asset is tied up and the seller has no right to sell to anyone else.

The reasons for selecting the executory contract to elaborate conflict blocking are threefold. First, two of the most common transactions lawyers are engaged to do, and students need to learn, the *real-property conveyance* and the *purchase of a company*, involve executory contracts. Secondly, the steps involved in the executory contract are uniquely designed to block conflict, mirroring those in the problem-solving process. Thirdly, many of the blocking solutions used in these transactions are inventive and, therefore, merit a closer look.

Conveyancing and the problem-solving process

In a conveyance, from the buyer's standpoint, his or her main goal is to take good title to the property on agreed terms. After receiving instructions to achieve this, the buyer's lawyer then investigates facts to discover if the buyer is buying what was contemplated and if he or she is getting value for money. The value of real property is affected by many factors, both legal (*e.g.* issues relating to title, zoning, planning, building) and factual (*e.g.* the physical state of the property).

In the fact-investigation stage, an all-important conflict-blocking area for the buyer's lawyer is questions of legal title. The lawyer must examine the title to the property, make other inquiries and ensure that by the time the transaction is completed the buyer is getting good title. To block conflicts in this area, lawyers must be able to apply case and statute law to identify legal issues that may constitute a title problem. In any property transaction, lawyers should have at their disposal a checklist of all major title problems and an inventory of standard solutions for blocking them.

A simple example: the seller may have had a mortgage registered against the property. To provide the buyer with good title this mortgage must be discharged. The problem is that the seller usually does not have the money to discharge the mortgage before completion. The standard solution is that the seller's lawyer and buyer's lawyer agree to hold back part of the sale proceeds from the seller in order to discharge the mortgage.

More complex issues can arise. Construction of the building to be purchased could be in breach of planning laws and the legal consequence may be that the planning department has the right to dismantle the whole or part of a building and charge the costs to the owner. This risk would be unacceptable to most buyers. In this situation, the buyer's lawyer could then negotiate with the seller's lawyer. They could agree that construction comply with legal requirements and a certificate of compliance from the planning department be provided prior to completion.

This is called *setting up a condition precedent*. The buyer's lawyer would include a provision in the agreement that obtaining the certificate prior to the scheduled completion is a condition (precedent) to completion. The non-fulfilment of the condition would provide the buyer with an escape, which is why conditions precedent are sometimes referred to as *escape clauses*. Setting up conditions precedent is critical to many types of executory contract. Indeed, one of the reasons for using an executory contract to complete a transaction is so that conditions which are not met at the time of the agreement can be met by the time of completion.

The lawyer can use other types of blocking tactics, such as renegotiating the purchase price, or modifying the seller's warranties or representations in the standard-form purchase agreement. Of course, the buyer has other options. If during the legal-issue identification stage, the buyer finds that certain issues are creating risks or obstacles that he or she does not even want to try overcoming, then the buyer can instruct the lawyer to abort the transaction by not entering into an agreement at all or by terminating one if it already exists.

If, however, the buyer does decide to go ahead and blocking action is implemented, the buyer's lawyer would later complete the transaction by transferring title to, and possession of, the property to the buyer and handing over the purchase money to the seller. At the delicate moment of completion, lawyers fulfil a special blocking function. They can act as escrow agents, taking money from buyers and holding it for sellers, but not putting it directly into their hands, until they have received ironclad assurances that all conditions will be met.

Because lawyers are insured for negligence and are subject to court supervision, the legal risk to clients in these situations is low. Here, one is reminded of Vonnegut's magic moment during which "a man has surrendered a treasure, and during which the man who is due to receive it has not yet done so." During this moment the sorcerer/lawyer is performing no magic. Behind the scenes, he or she is just a conflict-blocker/escrow agent who, for a fee, provides comfort and security while both money and property are in transit.

As a process of problem solving the real-property conveyance is depicted in Figure 8-1 on page 117.

Purchase of a company and blocking solutions

The purchase of all the shares of a small company is another example of the use of the executory contract. The stages of the process are much like those in a conveyance. As in a real-property conveyance, buyers need to know precisely what they are buying and they need firm assurances to that effect. From the buyer's standpoint, it is necessary to do fact investigation prior to settling the terms of the agreement and to ensure issues, including those raised by the investigation, are resolved in the agreement and before completion. These are both legal and non-legal issues, and lawyers are able to resolve these with a variety of blocking solutions.

As with conveyancing lawyers, business lawyers have a lengthy inventory of these solutions. Several examples discussed below high-light the inventiveness of the unknown lawyers who put them together. They are as follows: setting up conditions precedent, using non-competition agreements, and using contingent pricing.

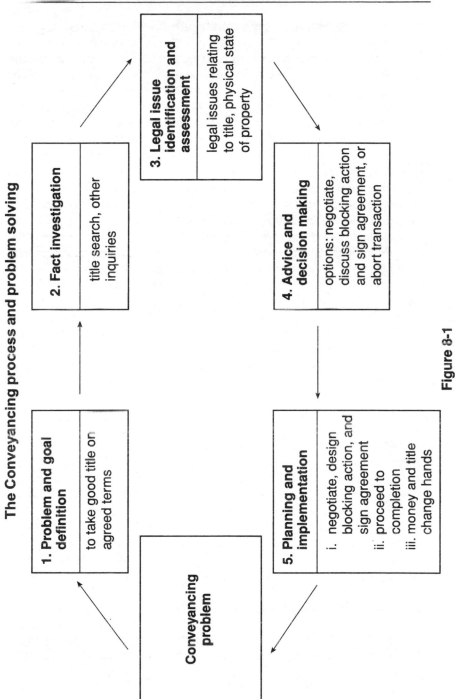

The Conveyancing process and problem solving

1. Problem and goal definition
to take good title on agreed terms

2. Fact investigation
title search, other inquiries

3. Legal issue identification and assessment
legal issues relating to title, physical state of property

4. Advice and decision making
options: negotiate, discuss blocking action and sign agreement, or abort transaction

5. Planning and implementation
i. negotiate, design blocking action, and sign agreement
ii. proceed to completion
iii. money and title change hands

Conveyancing problem

Figure 8-1

Setting up conditions precedent

When a client buys a company certain conditions precedent must be set up without which the shares of that company may be worthless. But how do lawyers know which conditions precedent? They might know from experience that the purchase of certain kinds of companies requires certain kinds of conditions to protect the buyer. Or the client may say right at the start that one of the goals of the transaction is to ensure a particular condition is met. For example, the client may only want to buy the company if the managing director continues on in that capacity for a certain period.

The most systematic way to set up conditions precedent necessary to protect the client is to use a well-designed plan with standard procedures and documents, preferably used for purchases of similar businesses. To set up conditions precedent properly, the lawyer has to do a thorough and vigorous fact investigation. One standard procedure buyers' lawyers use in the investigation is the delivery of a *shopping list* to the seller's lawyer. This shopping list is a lengthy list of requests to produce various pieces of information and documents about the company's business and its prospects. The more relevant information the buyer can get, the less risk it faces in the acquisition. Examples of information sought include financial statements, employee lists and employee contracts, property ownership details, guarantees, and mortgages or other charges given by the company.[1]

Another item usually asked for is licenses held by the company. Another is leases under which the company is a lessee. The transfer of both is often dependent on *third-party consents*. In other words, if the ownership of a company changes hands, for a licence or lease to go with it, the written consent of the licensing authority or the lessor may have to be obtained. When documents and other information are flushed out in the fact-investigation stage, the lawyer scrutinises them and creates a list of third-party consents that need to be obtained prior to completion. These can then be addressed in the agreement stage by setting up conditions precedent. Finally, before or at completion, the seller can produce the third-party consents in order to fulfil the conditions. Without these consents it may literally be impossible for the buyer to carry on the business and the company may be worthless.

Using non-competition agreements to block conflicts

Another problem that may emerge in acquisition agreements is how to prevent the seller from starting up the same or similar business in competition with the newly-purchased business. Much of the value of the newly purchased business is its *goodwill*, an intangible asset that depends on its prestige and friendly relations with customers. If, after selling the business, the seller immediately starts up another business in the same area, attracting the same customers, the value of the newly-purchased business could plummet. The conflict blocker has to ensure that the buyer is not confronted with this kind of competition after completion otherwise losses will surely follow. Lawyers solve this problem by getting their clients to enter into a non-competition agreement.

In the non-competition agreement, the seller agrees not to compete with the newly purchased business for a certain number of years and within a certain area. Under the common law, non-competition agreements (or restrictive covenants as they are sometimes called) are ordinarily treated as restraints of trade. As such, they are void as contrary to public policy. The courts, however, have upheld restraints of trade where they were found to be reasonable as between the parties and where they were not injurious to the public interest. In practical terms, this means that the courts will strike out agreements if they restrain trade too widely. If the restraint lasts for too long, or if the trade restrained is too broadly defined, or if the geographical area in which the trade is restrained is too large, the court will strike out the offending provisions as being unenforceable.

In drafting an enforceable restrictive covenant, lawyers need to remember to limit the conditions so that they go no further than is necessary to adequately protect the business sold.[2] But the problem is, what does "no further than necessary" mean? Judges had plenty of room to interpret this notion but little leeway when applying it. Take this example: what if a specific non-competition provision restrains trade in a particular business in the whole of Hong Kong? The seller then opens up a competing business in the district of Kowloon, the buyer sues to stop the seller and the court decides restraint throughout Hong Kong is too wide. In that event, the court would have no alternative but to strike out the provision and the buyer might be at risk of losing its investment. The court would have little leeway to amend or rectify the provision to reduce the size of the restricted area from the territory of Hong Kong to, say, the district of Kowloon.

Lawyers have devised a solution to this problem: draft the provision in severable pieces so that judges can strike out a piece at a time without demolishing the whole. For example, in relation to geographical area, they would not draft the provision as restraining trade in the territory of Hong Kong only, but as restraining trade in ever-widening areas or concentric circles:

1. Each Seller covenants and agrees with the buyer that he will not at any time....in any manner whatsoever carry on or be engaged in....any business or any part thereof presently carried on by the Company within any of the areas described in paragraph 2 herein...

2. The areas referred to in paragraph 1 are the following:
   (a) within a radius of one kilometre of the premises of the company;
   (b) within a radius of four kilometeres of the premises of the company;
   (c) within Hong Kong Island;
   (d) within Kowloon and Hong Kong Island;
   (e) within the territory of Hong Kong.

3. Each provision of this Agreement is declared to constitute a separate and distinct covenant and to be severable from all other such separate and distinct covenants........

If the provision is subsequently challenged by the seller, the court need not strike out the entire provision as being too wide, but may choose to strike out only the wider circles of restriction, saving the narrower ones for the buyer to rely on. This ingenious blocking action greatly reduces the risk to buyers of losing the value of their investment.

Using contingent pricing to block conflicts

Well-structured transactions handled by lawyers can clearly protect clients from suffering losses. But these transactions can work even more subtly, for example, by helping buyers and sellers design rational mechanisms to determine the price of a particular asset. The corporate acquisition once more provides a good example. When the asset is a residential house or flat, lawyers usually do not have to get involved in price-setting, since buyers and sellers can get enough information about the asset through the real-estate market. But when the asset is a business with a future stream of income, pricing can become much more difficult. In these circumstances the price of the business may be contingent on future events, and buyer and seller will have very different ideas of what those future events might produce. The seller usually believes future income (or the increase in *net assets*) is likely to be higher than the buyer's estimate, and so will insist on a higher price for the business than the buyer.

When the parties are negotiating a corporate-acquisition agreement, many uncertainties cloud decisions about price, and the expected increase in the net assets of the company as a result of income generated after the agreement is signed is a major uncertainty. This is complicated by the fact that the preparation of company accounts to determine the value of the net assets on any given day cannot be completed until some time after the completion date. To address this uncertainty lawyers often include in the corporate-acquisition agreement provisions such as these:

(a) If the net assets are less than £2 million the seller will pay the buyer within seven days after determination of the net assets a sum equal to the amount of such shortfall but with no interest thereon.

(b) If the net assets are greater than £2 million, the buyer will pay the seller within seven days after determination of the net assets a sum equal to the amount of such excess but with no interest thereon.

Because of these provisions, the buyer will pay most of the purchase price on the completion date which will be adjusted some time later according to the above formula. The adjustment will depend on the auditors' accounts and calculation of the net assets as of the completion date, although these accounts will not be ready until some time later.

The conflict the buyer and seller have is not about future events that might have legal consequences; the conflict is in their expectations about the company's future income.[3] *This contingent-price* provision solves the problem in a way that tends to block potential conflict by bringing their expectations into line with each other.

This is a solution to what is essentially a non-legal problem, that is, how to put a price on future income or losses. Because it is implemented after completion it protects the buyer who might otherwise fear the seller could, with impunity, run down the assets before completion. It protects the seller by ensuring the buyer does not get an income windfall that has not been paid for. The beauty of this provision lies in the way it uses the passage of time to transform uncertainty about price into greater certainty.[4]

2. BLOCKING CONFLICTS IN NEGOTIATION

The above examples of standard solutions are used to block conflicts in acquisition transactions. An infinite number of modifications to these are possible, depending on the parties' goals and bargaining power. They are usually modified through negotiations.

Negotiations in conflict-blocking situations are similar to playing-out negotiations in one important respect. As with their playing-out counterparts, conflict-blocking negotiators usually negotiate on the basis of principle, that is by appealing to objective standards and precedents. Let us continue with the example of the corporate acquisition. The price paid for the business may be determined to a large extent by bargaining power, but the individual or subsidiary terms of the acquisition agreement are usually negotiated and drafted by lawyers. Although the outcome of these negotiations may also be affected by such factors as bargaining power, lawyers negotiate these subsidiary terms largely by reference to principle. They invoke existing precedents and persuade each other with reasoned elaboration.[5]

The negotiation of warranties in the corporate-acquisition agreement is a good example to illustrate how precedent and reasoned elaboration help to determine the terms of the agreement. In the agreement, the seller is obliged to make warranties in relation to the company — for example, in relation to the assets, liabilities, accounts, employees, accuracy of information supplied and so forth. Sometimes the warranties are intended to be met before completion and meeting them, as we have seen, is made a condition precedent to completion. Sometimes the warranties are intended to survive completion and the seller assumes long-term liability for these warranties. Without some kind of blocking action the seller's liability in relation to these warranties could be unlimited as to length of time and amount. That is why sellers' lawyers want to insert provisions to limit that liability. A simple liability-limit clause might look like this:

> The liability of the seller in respect of all the warranties shall not, in respect of all breaches thereof, in any event exceed $.................

What amount should the buyer and seller fill in? How would they negotiate the amount? The buyer's lawyer might object to the seller introducing such a clause in the first place. The seller's lawyer might then try to limit the amount. After some wrangling the seller's lawyer might say, "Look, my client will agree to a limit equal to the price your client is paying for all the shares, but no higher."

With this proposal, the seller's lawyer would have two strong supporting arguments that would be hard to resist. The first is based on reasoned elaboration: "My client, the seller, should not assume more potential loss than gain in a sale transaction. In other words, why should my client give up the limited-liability status of a shareholder to take on *unlimited* liability under an acquisition agreement? His liability should be no greater than when he was a shareholder." The second argument is based on precedent. The seller's lawyer can say: "This is a standard clause; it's used all the time. The onus is on you to prove why it should not be used in this case."[6]

Obviously, to negotiate competently on the basis of principle, lawyers must know what the precedents are, how they were developed and how to both defend and attack them. This knowledge was referred to at the end of the last chapter as *knowing the plans*. Just as the conflict-player must *know the law and facts* to negotiate on the basis of principle so the conflict-player must *know the plans* to be able to do the same.

In conflict-blocking negotiations, the plans usually contain many items to negotiate and, unlike playing-out problems in which the goal is to win or settle, the blocking goal is usually to complete the deal within a limited time. Conflict-blocking negotiations, therefore, often require much more give and take so that the deal will go forward. Lawyers need to give on one item and take on another. The competent negotiator who wants the negotiation to result in a completed deal, yet still uphold the client's interests, needs to prioritise the client's goals carefully, selecting those items that can be conceded and those that require more competitive negotiating. The lawyer must also be prepared to use reasoned elaboration and precedent to support the arguments for selecting those items.

But lawyers often need to go beyond principled negotiation into the realm of creative problem solving, otherwise deals are at risk of being held up by rigid thinking. In conflict-blocking negotiations, the opportunities for creative problem-solving are numerous because many items have to be reviewed and negotiated and the parties are usually highly motivated to make a deal. In these situations, as in the will problem, lawyers need to know how to meet the parties' goals by using the appropriate structures. James Freund provides a good example.[7] An acquisition agreement is being negotiated. The seller's first quarter financial statements (unaudited) are going to become available after the agreement is signed but before completion. Naturally the buyer wants to ensure these financial statements show a solid performance. So the buyer's lawyer has presented a draft agreement that contains a seller's warranty, intended to survive completion, in relation to these not-yet-prepared statements. The warranty is just as strong and contains just as many promises as for the already prepared and audited year-end financial statements that the buyer has seen.

The seller's lawyer does not want the client to agree to that warranty because it would mean the client would have to indemnify the buyer forever for errors in financial statements that the seller has not seen and which are not even prepared. The buyer then becomes suspicious: "Why won't the seller give the warranty? Is the first quarter a disaster?" The deal is on the verge of breakdown.

But then Freund demonstrates how the problem can be solved. He looks closely at what the parties' goals really are to see if they can be reconciled. The buyer's goal, he reasons, is not that he has to have a warranty in relation to the first-quarter statements that survives completion; his real concern is that the first quarter-statements do not reflect a drastic downtrend in profits before he has even bought the business.[8] For his part, the seller does not want to sign an open-ended warranty on unseen documents. But because he is familiar with his company's operations, he is confident that the first-quarter profits are going to be strong.

Freund's solution is to meet both parties' goals, as he has now redefined them, by deleting the warranty and having the seller demonstrate his confidence in the first-quarter profits in some other way. The way Freund chooses is to set up a condition precedent to completion: if the first-quarter statements are not at least as good as in the previous quarter the buyer is not obliged to complete.[9] Both buyer and seller accept this solution and the problem is solved.

3. THE BLOCKING ENDGAME

Lawyers sometimes cannot succeed in blocking every potential conflict. No matter how deep their knowledge and skills, they cannot block conflicts when people are intent on fighting. With executory contracts in particular, a blocking problem can easily turn into a playing-out problem. With real-property conveyancing, this can occur in a variety of situations. After an agreement is signed, but before completion, anxiety can sway buyers and sellers who sometimes look for ways to escape their obligations. This is when lawyers move into the blocking endgame.

One of the most common situations is when property markets are volatile — when prices are going rapidly up or down. When prices are going up, sellers can change their minds in a matter of days or even hours. They often want to escape from agreements. When they are going down, buyers can be just as fickle. Sellers can claim buyers have not performed their obligations on time and buyers can claim sellers have not met conditions set out in the agreement. At the end of the blocking process, in the twilight zone between blocking and playing, lawyers make last-ditch attempts aggressively to protect their clients. Consider these two letters:

Today
By Fax

Dear Seller's Lawyer

Re: 42–3 Hobart

We write to confirm our client's position in this matter, although he has already made it abundantly clear to your client. The representation made by your client that the success of his rezoning application was only a "formality," appears not to be true. All parties knew that rezoning was a condition precedent to completion. It may not have been explicitly stated in the agreement, but our correspondence, particularly your letter of May 10, bears this out.

At any rate, neither we or the buyer has received satisfactory evidence of rezoning as referred to in your letter and the completion date is one week from today. Accordingly, therefore, unless your client can produce to us the requested evidence by the close of business on the date scheduled for completion, he will be in breach of the April 14 agreement. Our client will then be entitled to rescind it and to demand the return of his deposit.

On behalf of our client, we expressly reserve all his rights.

Yours sincerely

Buyer's Lawyer

Figure 8-2

Today
By Fax

Dear Buyer's Lawyer

Re: 42–3 Hobart

Thank you for your fax dated today. As you and your client know the rezoning application is in progress and our client has been given written assurances it will go forward very soon — probably within a couple of weeks, though it could take longer. We do not understand why these assurances are not satisfactory to you. Final approval, as you must know, is only a formality. And you and your client were both well aware a delay in obtaining final approval could occur.

Although we are confident that final approval is not required under the April 14 agreement, both as a courtesy and as a precaution, we have asked you several times for an extension of the completion date, but you have continued unreasonably to refuse our several requests for an extension. We repeat the request made three days ago in the same terms.

Yours sincerely,

Seller's lawyer

Figure 8-3

Obviously, a conflict is brewing and the lawyers are creating a self-serving record in these letters to argue the correctness of their position, to intimidate the other side and to give their clients leverage in the event the conflict boils over into litigation. The buyer does not want to complete because prices are falling and the buyer's lawyer has been instructed to extricate him from the deal. Hence the lawyers are either in the last stages of blocking or are beginning the process of playing out the conflict. They must engage in the process with delicacy. One wrong move could precipitate litigation; one wrong word could count as evidence against the client at some future trial. In an exercise such as this, lawyers need to have thorough knowledge of the relevant areas of contract law, they must know how to apply them to the facts and they must be able to put their arguments clearly and forcefully in writing.

For example, in the letter to the seller's lawyer, the buyer's lawyer was careful not to repudiate the agreement before the completion date otherwise his client could be accused of an unjustified *anticipatory breach*, that is, making a positive statement before the completion date that he will not carry out the terms of the contract. Knowing how to apply the law also includes knowing how to appear reasonable, since "reasonable behaviour" is often a critical element for a judge in deciding a contractual dispute. For example, the seller's lawyer was careful to assert that the written assurances received to date do satisfy the conditions, but he still offered to bend over backwards by asking for an extension of the completion date several times.

With falling property prices, the consequences of a wrongly-worded letter at this juncture can be serious. If the conflict is litigated and goes to trial, a successful seller could force the buyer to buy at a price much higher than the market value prevailing at the time of trial. And a successful buyer could save a great deal of money at the expense of the seller.

4. BLOCKING AND COMPETENCE

During the *legal-issue identification and assessment stage*, the lawyer can identify a legal issue that may present a risk of potential conflict for the client. The lawyer then has to decide whether to try to block the conflict. If it involves a simple step such as drafting another clause, the answer is usually to go ahead. But if the inclusion of that clause depends on successful negotiations with the opposite party, the lawyer must evaluate whether the cost in time, money and risk is worth the effort. The lawyer has to decide whether to block or not to block the potential conflict.

In its most common form, this dilemma involves a third party. To make the decision, the lawyer usually needs some assurance from a third party so that the transaction can proceed safely. Sometimes this assurance, such as a tax opinion, a surveyor's certificate, or an approval from a government agency can take a long time, or be expensive to obtain.

At other times, the lawyer may be wiser not to seek the assurance because the third party may refuse to provide it or may be alerted about a transaction that might never have come to its notice if it had not been contacted in the first place.

How conflict-blocking lawyers deal with this kind of dilemma provides a useful indicator of their problem-solving ability.[10]

Suppose, for example, that the transaction may need the approval of a regulatory agency. Lawyers who do not know that agency approval may be necessary would be at the lowest level of a competence hierarchy. Unable even to identify the relevant legal issue, these lawyers would not be in a position to competently advise the client.

At the next level of competence would be those lawyers who identify the issue but do not evaluate the risks, make no decision but then proceed with the transaction anyway.

Third from the bottom are lawyers who spot the issue, realise a risk is involved and decide immediately to seek agency approval. They may succeed in blocking the potential conflict, but are heedless of the new risk that the agency might not approve a transaction that, but for the lawyer's decision, might never have come to its attention. Not having evaluated risk effectively, these lawyers are in no position to analyse the options.

At the top of the competence hierarchy are lawyers who know that the agency should be contacted in certain circumstances.[11] To advise the client properly and make a calculated decision, the lawyer has to do a thorough risk evaluation and analysis of options. The lawyer should look at factors such as when, and in what circumstances, to notify the agency, as well as its likely position in this particular case.[12] Having made a decision in consultation with the client, the high-level problem solver would proceed to the final stage of completion, implementing it with subtlety and good judgment.

MINIMISING UNCERTAINTY

Whereas conflict-players solve problems by managing uncertainty, building a case and improving the odds until conflict is resolved, conflict-blockers solve problems by minimising uncertainty with intricate structures such as executory contracts, creatively negotiated solutions and careful, researched advice to clients. The conflict-blocker meets important needs in society. Whether they involve borrowing or lending money, entering in to commercial contracts, planning a trust or will, or buying and selling expensive assets, it takes a high level of skill to identify issues and design plans that successfully block conflict. Perhaps Vonnegut's suggestion to law students that "a lawyer should be looking for situations where large amounts of money are about to change hands" should be recast into advice for clients rather than students: if you are involved in a transaction where a large amount of money is about to change hands, hire a competent conflict-blocking lawyer who knows how to keep it from getting lost in the shuffle.

[1] Standard documents were provided by Tony Wales of Turner Kenneth Brown.

[2] 47 Halsbury's Laws (4th ed.) para. 24.

[3] Ronald Gilson, "Value Creation By Business Lawyers", (1984) 94 *Yale Law Journal* 239–313 at 263.

[4] *ibid.*

[5] Melvin Eisenberg, "Private Ordering Through Negotiation: Dispute-Settlement and Rule-Making" (1976), 89 *Harvard Law Review*, 637–681 at 665–666.

[6] James Freund says that the parties, of course, can agree to a lower limit, although it may sometimes be difficult for the seller's lawyer to negotiate it. Buyers' lawyers, however, will usually agree to the "purchase-price" limit because the likelihood of damages exceeding the purchase price is remote: see James Freund, *Anatomy of a Merger* (Law Journal Press; New York, 1975), p.376.

[7] James Freund, *Lawyering: A Realistic Approach To Legal Practice,* (Law Journal Seminars-Press, Inc., New York, 1979), pp.204–205.

[8] *ibid.*

[9] *ibid.*

[10] *ibid.*, p.242.

[11] *ibid.*

[12] *ibid.*

CHAPTER 9

ETHICS AND THE VALUE OF LAWYERING

ETHICAL PROBLEMS

Legal problem solving can be both a linear and a flexible process. The more experienced and confident a lawyer is, the more the lawyer can use these two facets of problem solving. One dimension of solving problems that requires flexible thinking, no matter how experienced the practitioner, is professional ethics. In the world of legal conflict, where the stakes are high and the desire to win is strong, some lawyers may be tempted to take the easy way out. Like all legal problems, lawyers' ethical problems involve conflict, not conflict between people, but conflict that usually sets professional duties and interests against each other. Common ethical problems involve three major types of conflict: between different professional duties; between professional duty and various interests; and between different interests.

Conflict between different duties

Consider the case of Patrick Meehan. In 1969, Meehan was convicted of murder and sentenced to life imprisonment in a Scottish jail. The murder charge arose out of a burglary in which an elderly couple named Ross were tied up and robbed of several thousand pounds in takings from Mr Ross' bingo hall. Mrs Ross died later in hospital after having remained tied up the whole weekend. A Glasgow jury found Mr Meehan guilty on the basis of circumstantial and voice-identification evidence by a majority of nine to six.

Meehan's solicitor, Mr Beltrami, was convinced of Meehan's innocence and continued to work for him, searching for exculpatory evidence. Two or three years later, a Glasgow criminal named Tank McGuinness, for whom Beltrami was also acting, confessed to Beltrami that he was in fact responsible for the murder, not Meehan. Because of his duty of confidentiality to McGuinness, Beltrami was unable to reveal to anyone this evidence which would have been helpful in freeing Meehan.[1]

The advantage of upholding the confidentiality rule is that clients can feel secure about communicating openly and honestly with their lawyers. This facilitates the flow of information to lawyers so that they can do their jobs properly. The legal system would be undermined if it could not guarantee open and honest communication between lawyer and client. Concern about the system being weakened is the reason why lawyers respect and abide by the rule.

In this particular situation, Beltrami's dilemma was that his duty of confidentiality to McGuinness was in direct conflict with his duty to act in Meehan's best interests. But Beltrami knew he had to follow the rule that when a client communicates information to a lawyer, even about past criminal acts, the communication cannot be disclosed unless the client consents or special circumstances exist. He had to let his duty of confidentiality prevail.

It cannot have been an easy decision, and either way the lawyer would have to bear a heavy burden. Even though Beltrami must have had realised that the confidentiality rule would probably supersede Meehan's right to vindication, he must still have had an agonising time deciding to adhere to the rule when another client was being so unjustly punished. In one American case, a lawyer whose client disclosed to him the whereabouts of her husband's remains decided to reveal this to the authorities. His client's later conviction was overturned because the rule of confidentiality had been breached.[2] This lawyer must also have had a painful struggle with his conscience before breaking the rule. In addition, the lack of judicial support for what he did must have been devastating to him personally and professionally.

As for Beltrami, his story ended on a more positive note. His client, McGuinness, was killed in a street brawl, so Beltrami was able to release details of the Ross murder confession. Meehan was eventually released.

The issue of confidentiality frequently presents ethical dilemmas for lawyers, not perhaps as dramatic as the one just described, but just as likely to create enormous pressures for lawyers. In an Australian child custody dispute, a mother, in violation of a court order giving custody to the father, kept the child with her at a secret address. At a later time, she instructed a solicitor, Mr Lees, to act for her in relation to the matrimonial home. She told her lawyer how to get in touch with her but told him to keep it confidential.

The Family Court ordered Mr Lees to disclose the address, but he refused and took the matter to the Australian High Court.[3] The High Court stood by the Family Court, saying that Mr Lees' duty to his client did not extend so far as to further "an illegal object", that is, assisting her in continuing to disobey a court order. The High Court also said the welfare of the child was of such paramount concern that it must supersede any such duty. The High Court instructed Lees to disclose the address, and he did.

Mr Lees' approach to the problem, however, was both principled and well thought-out. Although he lost the confidentiality battle, he won the ethical war. At the beginning, when he was ordered by Family Court to reveal the information, he resisted by taking the matter to a higher court. He tried to uphold his professional duty of confidentiality even though he was ordered to release confidential information by the Family Court. By taking the case to a higher court, he was adopting a win-win strategy for solving the problem. If the court sided with him, then his client's interests would be protected. But if the court ruled against him, as it eventually did, then it would be the court compelling him to breach confidentiality; it would not be his choice. And in that event, he would still have demonstrated his determination to serve his client's interests to the best of his ability. Mr Lees resolved the conflict between his professional duty to his client and his duty to protect a child's welfare by giving the problem to the court to solve.

Conflict between duty and interest

It is not often that lawyers can throw ethical problems in the court's lap. Usually, they have to make the important decisions themselves. Ethical problems frequently arise because, as an officer of the court, the lawyer owes duties to it. But these can easily conflict with the client's interest as well as the lawyer's. Problems associated with this issue can be difficult to solve. If they are not dealt with properly, they can lead to disaster.

One of the best known cases of lawyers misleading the court and paying dearly for it occurred in New York in the late 1970s. Berkey Photo, a small photographic-products company sued Kodak, the giant film and camera company, for anti-trust violations. The case was extensively covered and the focus of much media attention.[4] Berkey claimed that Kodak had used monopolistic tactics to pressure smaller competitors out of the photographic-products market. Berkey said that Kodak introduced new products designed to be incompatible with their competitors and devoured smaller companies in an acquisition strategy to gain dominance in the market.

Kodak, in its defence, said that its market success was due to technological innovation, not predatory practices. It had an arguable defence and plenty of evidence. But because of an ethical lapse on the part of Kodak's lawyers, Berkey managed to get the jury on its side, winning a staggering award of U.S.$113 million.

Acting for Kodak was a hard-working, ambitious team of about 30 lawyers from the prestigious New York firm of Donovan Leisure Newton & Irvine. An important part of the Kodak defence was based on the testimony of an expert witness, Yale economics professor Merton Peck, who would testify that the key to Kodak's success was its innovation, not its monopolistic strategy of acquiring smaller competitors.

In 1974, however, Professor Peck wrote to Donovan Leisure stating that, after much analysis, he was now uncertain about the real reason for Kodak's success. He was unsure as to whether the acquisition strategy (as opposed to innovation) was in fact responsible for Kodak's dominance in the marketplace. His lengthy report, which obviously would weaken his testimony on this issue if ever revealed, was later to become the infamous exhibit 666 at the trial, one of two smoking guns that caused Kodak to lose millions.

The reason it became a smoking gun was because, until a crucial moment in the trial, it had been concealed by one of Donovan Leisure's lawyers. Despite an order directing discovery of all of Peck's interim reports, Mahlon Perkins, a senior partner, had concealed the Peck report and misled the court about the whereabouts of other discoverable documents. He said under oath they had been inadvertently discarded, even though they were sitting in his office, a fact about which his young associate, Joseph Fortenberry, is alleged to have reminded him by whispering in his ear while Perkins was testifying on this point.

The denouement came when Peck was cross-examined by Berkey's lawyer, Alvin M. Stein. Stein asked Peck if there were in existence any documents "on this matter" prepared by Peck prior to April 1975. When Peck replied evasively asking Stein to define "on this matter", Stein, a brilliant, intuitive trial lawyer, knew he was on to something. He persisted in his questioning, extracting an admission that such a document did exist. When it was ultimately produced, Stein was able to cross-examine Professor Peck with crushing effectiveness, demonstrating how his views about the reasons for Kodak's dominance in the marketplace had changed. Stein utterly destroyed Peck's credibility. Mahlon Perkins eventually confessed he had concealed documents and the Kodak case collapsed in front of the jury.

The fallout from the trial was catastrophic, perhaps more so for Mahlon Perkins than for Kodak or Donovan Leisure. Although Kodak and Donovan Leisure both lost a great deal of money, Mr Perkins served one month in jail for criminal contempt of court. His career and reputation were ruined. As for the young associate who whispered the truth in Perkin's ear, Fortenberry was passed over for partnership at the firm and applied for many jobs at other firms without success.[5] Eventually he found a job with the government in Washington. As this case illustrates, when the duty to behave ethically conflicts with the desire to win for the client at all costs, some lawyers can find it difficult to achieve an acceptable resolution to the problem.

Conflict between different interests

Like many ethical problems, *Berkey v. Kodak* is really about how
self-interest can conflict with, and impinge on, professional duty. In
professional practice, self-interest can enter into almost every decision.
Lawyers need to be aware of how self-interest can easily dominate a
situation. They need to be vigilant and exert the necessary self-control to
stop this from happening. This does not mean, however, that where duty
and self-interest conflict, lawyers must disregard self-interest
completely and blindly follow duty. They need to look for ways to
balance the two, keeping in mind that serving the client is the most
important objective.

One lawyer who was able to achieve this explains:

I was acting for two defendants, a building contractor and a
small-time developer being sued in a fatal accident case. Both the
developer and the contractor were underinsured. In addition, I
suspected something was wrong with their development permit. The
deceased's father was suing my clients for damages for negligence
caused when the deceased was killed in an accident on a construction
site managed by the contractor and owned by the developer. The
deceased was a young messenger delivering a sub-contractor's
invoice to the construction manager. He was driving a motorcycle
quite fast and, unfortunately, drove straight into a ditch that had not
been properly covered. It was after working hours and getting dark.
When the motorcycle went into the ditch the messenger was hurled
into the air and, unfortunately, broke his neck.

Our defence was that the motorcyclist was driving too fast. The
plaintiff claimed that the site was unsafe. There was one witness who
saw the accident, but only from a distance of about 50 yards. I could
not understand why the client's watchman had not seen anything and
had not given a statement to the police. He should have been at the
entrance to the site. I went to see him myself.

He was nervous, but still forthcoming. Not only had he seen every
detail of the accident, but when the messenger came on to the site, he
had *warned* him emphatically about the ditch and even pointed it out
to him. The messenger ignored the warning and sped on. The
watchman hadn't said anything to the police because he had been told
by his developer boss, who was in a terrible panic at the time, not to
say he had seen the accident or, for that matter, anything. I think the
developer was panicked about the status of the development permit or
about conditions on the site. So the police took no statement from the
watchman. He refused to give me a written statement and said that if I

wanted him to be a witness I would have to subpoena him. In my view, he was a credible witness with a good memory and an eye for detail but, without a written statement, his testimony would be unpredictable.

I was in a quandary. The developer who told the watchman to say nothing and the building contractor were both my clients, but they clearly had conflicting interests. If I called the watchman as a witness to show that the messenger was largely responsible for his own negligence this would greatly diminish both defendants' liability for damages, but would increase the likelihood of the developer being charged with criminal obstruction of justice — a serious charge. He might also feel more exposed about the development permit problem.

Since they had both signed a joint retainer agreement allowing for sharing of all information and confidences, I called them both in to the office to discuss the matter. The contractor was quite angry with the developer for silencing the watchman and, naturally, wanted him called as a witness. Then the developer started blaming the contractor for not taking out proper insurance and keeping the site in a mess. They got into an argument.

At that point, because of the intensity of the conflict, I could have referred them to different lawyers. That is how many lawyers quite properly deal with conflicts of interest of this type. But I wanted to avoid losing them as clients. I realised I could keep both clients if they could reach an agreement between themselves and if I could settle the fatal accident claim. So I decided to try this approach for a little while to see if it might work.

I interviewed them both, listening and probing, to see if a working agreement could be reached between them. While some of their interests were in conflict, some seemed to make a nice fit. For one thing, they had both done business together for several years and had made a fair amount of money. For another, they could see that if this matter were settled amicably they could continue to do business. I could also see that the developer felt very badly about the death of the messenger. Finally, after two meetings, they agreed that if the watchman was not called as a witness, the developer would pay 70 per cent of any settlement and the contractor would pay 30 per cent, up to a ceiling.

I drew up a letter of agreement between them which they signed and advised them in covering letters to seek independent legal advice in the event the plaintiff's lawyer made an offer they could accept. They instructed me to proceed to negotiate with the plaintiff's lawyer. If I could not reach a settlement they would have to reconsider their options.

After several rounds of negotiations, the plaintiff's lawyer did make an acceptable offer. Each of my clients did obtain independent legal advice on the arrangements, a settlement was reached, and though no one was happy about the young man dying, my clients felt as if both they and the father had reached a fair settlement.

Of course, lawyers can get into trouble when they act for two or more clients whose interests conflict. If clients' interests conflict, the lawyer's decision to benefit one client may hurt the other. This means breaching professional duty to one of them. If the case of the deceased messenger had gone to trial, the lawyer could not realistically have acted for both defendants, especially if one of them had wanted to call the watchman as a witness and the other did not. Not having gone to trial, the lawyer could still have referred the clients to different lawyers to solve the conflict-of-interest problem. This would have been a safe, but not necessarily the most desirable, solution. If lawyers had to advise clients to see other lawyers every time a conflict of interest arose, clients could hardly be well-served bouncing from lawyer to lawyer, and lawyers would frequently be escaping problems rather than confronting them.

In this case, the lawyer found a way to reconcile the conflict of interest not only between his clients, but also between himself and his clients. The reconciliation of duties and interests behind the scenes may not be as dramatic an ethical outcome as in the *Kodak*, or *Meehan* cases, but it nevertheless occurs every day in practice.

Confronting and solving ethical problems is a pervasive aspect of legal problem solving. Some lawyers respond poorly to this challenge, foregoing or forgetting self-control. Or they persuade themselves to view duties and interests in isolation from human beings and human needs. This last group of lawyers regards codes of professional conduct as sterile rules with shades of meaning to be legalistically interpreted, rather than as guideposts to ethical behaviour. Fortunately, most lawyers do not view their jobs this way. They make decisions on a daily basis carefully balancing duties and interests so that their client's problems are solved without sacrificing ethical principles.

THE VALUE OF PLAYING OUT CONFLICT

Even if lawyers' ethical decision-making sometimes seems highly specific to legal problems, it is still concerned with the broader moral issues of right and wrong. This involvement with right and wrong not only challenges lawyers problem-solving skill, it also provides them with regular opportunities to test their moral fibre as well as to observe others in testing situations. To thoughtful lawyers, this can add layers of meaning and greater depth to professional life, providing them with unexpected avenues of insight into themselves as well as into life's larger questions. In a way, practising law has the potential to provide meaningful life experience to those who take it seriously. This is obviously of great value to those practising law, but is what lawyers do of value for society as a whole?

Lawyers can, and do, make altruistic choices to help those who have suffered injustice. They help others by acting, without remuneration, for clients who cannot afford their services. They act for social causes such as taking polluters to court, representing the physically or mentally handicapped, advocating children's or women's rights, and advancing the rights of consumers. Many act as equalisers, representing those with little power in society against those with a great deal of power.

Lawyers are also in a unique position to help others in a broader sense. They can use the skills of listening, empathy, and communication not only to help clients achieve their goals, but to enhance their own role as helpers, improving the human condition by making connections with and serving other human beings.[6]

The fact that lawyers can choose to work toward achieving ends that society regards as good, however, does not alter the perspective of many people who do not respect lawyers. A lot of people, for instance, do not have much respect for personal injury lawyers, although they can act as equalisers for clients who have been injured. In some countries such as the United States and Canada, where contingency fees are allowed, the system of permitting lawyers to finance lawsuits and take a piece of the action arguably has resulted in huge economic and social costs to society. These criticisms revolve around the idea that lawyers in such a system are given large incentives to create disputes, exacerbate conflicts, claim injustice where there is none and drive up insurance premiums at the expense of everyone else.[7]

Since no legal system is perfect, it is vulnerable to exploitation by skilful lawyers. As the Attorney-General of California once said: "An incompetent attorney can delay a trial for years or months. A competent attorney can delay one even longer."[8] But even as people grudgingly admire those who exploit the system, they forget that too much exploitation can easily erode the system's integrity. When skilful conflict-players achieve bad ends for bad clients or when their actions as lawyers result in negative social or economic consequences, it undermines the image of the legal system. When wealthy litigants are able to defeat less wealthy ones in a trial not because their cause is just, but because they have more resources and skilled lawyers to fight with, it makes people distrustful of the system and the legal profession. And that has a detrimental effect on all of us.

When confronted with criticisms about the injustices of the legal system, conflict-players have three forceful responses: the rule-of-law response, the system-reform response and the process-evolution response.

The rule-of-law response

A common justification for the injustices that result from the exploitation of the legal system by skilful players is that the occasional injustice is a small price to pay to maintain a system based on the rule of law. Everybody has heard the old saying that it's better that 10 guilty men should go free than that one innocent man should be convicted of an offence he did not commit. That a court verdict can be determined only in accordance with law and procedures formulated in advance is a fundamental aspect of the rule of law. When Rumpole, on getting an acquittal in front of the detestable Judge Bullingham muttered, "The natural malice of the Bull had been quelled by his instinctive respect for the law", Rumpole was paying tribute to the rule of law in action. Respect for the law and the way it works is ingrained not only in the system but in its participants, even if they are unpopular figures. They are the ones who make it work.

The rule of law, which includes features such as an independent, uncorrupt judiciary, the presumption that an accused is innocent until proven guilty beyond a reasonable doubt, clear laws that reflect society's values, and independent lawyers who regard clients as their first responsibility, is an ideology that many worship. If one believes in this ideology, then the value of what lawyers do is obvious. If a wrong is done to somebody, lawyers have the knowledge and skills to seek redress or to defend accusations according to law.

Others take the system for granted, perhaps forgetting when they criticise lawyers, how lawyers in authoritarian systems operate. These lawyers may deliberately do more harm than good for a client. As explained by law professors at the University of Havana, "the first job of the revolutionary lawyer is not to argue that his client is innocent, but rather to determine if his client is guilty and, if so, to seek the sanction that will best rehabilitate him."[9]

Even when authoritarianism comes to an end, however, the rule of law does not necessarily spring into life on its own. It needs time and nurturing to take root, and it needs lawyers to put it into practice. From this viewpoint, the rule of law is not just an ideology, an attitude or, as Rumpole suggested, an instinct to do what is right. It is a highly-sophisticated practice that requires well-trained practitioners to make it work. Players who play by the rules, even if they do exploit them to the hilt, are living proof that the rule of law works the way it should.

In a modern rule-of-law environment, the orderly resolution of conflicts is a critical social and economic necessity. The conflict-players' job is to resolve conflicts. If they do this to the client's satisfaction, then something of value has been achieved, if only because the client has not chosen to resolve it by violence or corruption.

The value that players create, however, goes beyond the benefits provided to individual clients. In civil disputes, when players take a case all the way to court, they create *precedents*. Precedents are an important source of law that provide guides to behaviour. Precedents save time and money for society because they signal what is considered appropriate legal behaviour and what is not. When people know what the precedents are the likelihood of their getting involved in destructive legal conflict is reduced.[10]

The system-reform response

Another response people give to criticisms of lawyers is to argue that the way to ensure the legal system serves its purpose is not to abandon it or blame lawyers for causing injustice, but to continue to push for reform of the system.

The civil-justice system, for example, has many weaknesses: it is too expensive; it often results in excessive delays; it can be unpredictable; it makes insufficient allowance for resource inequality which can exist between the litigants.[11] Perhaps the most likely, underlying reason for these problems is its adversary character—the premise that judges can sit back passively and make good decisions about what to do based on evidence and arguments put by opposing sides. One of the difficulties with this model is that judges do not see a great deal of the behind-the-scenes manoeuvring or concealment that lawyers and clients use to make winning moves.

Perhaps a more active hands-on role assumed by judges, or judicial officials, would alleviate some of the problems caused by the adversary system. Lord Woolf's very first recommendation in his interim report on the civil justice system in England and Wales states that "[t]here should be a fundamental transfer in the responsibility for the management of civil litigation from litigants and their legal advisers to the courts."[12]

Although it can be argued that the conflict-player's function is not to reform the system, but to do the best he or she can for clients within it, perhaps the player's relationship to the reform process needs to be changed. At present, lawyers generally facilitate the process by sitting on law reform commissions or on judge-led committees, donating their time and experience on a part-time basis. They are consulted and their opinions are sought. But they do not generally work as professional experts in legal-system reform. Reform is usually left to the judges, many of whom may not have fought cases for years. As a result, sometimes the reform process tends to lean toward procedural changes in order to convenience judges. It would probably benefit the system for the reform process to be professionalised, that is, for it to become a specialist vocation that attracts not only judges, but also experienced conflict-players.

In common law countries, some of the best of the conflict-players cap their careers by being elevated to the bench. But some of these people should be given the opportunity to move into a new and different branch of the judicial profession. Instead of becoming judges who solve the problems of litigants, they should be given the opportunity to work as specialists on solving the problems of the legal system, helping it progress toward a more efficient and humane system of justice. As conflict-players who have used — even legitimately exploited — the system to its limits, with their arsenal of litigation tactics and ruses, these lawyers would be in a unique position to reform the process. The best of them could be recruited to work in a full-time, professional capacity as "legal-system specialists." They can be transformed from legal problem solvers to legal-system problem solvers and be given recognition and status similar to that of judges.

The process-evolution response

Related to the system-reform response is the idea that, spurred by client need and lawyer creativity, the playing-out-conflict process is capable of evolving into a more just, humane process. If, as Lord Woolf says, the adversarial nature of the system is an obstacle to justice, then clients and lawyers can simply choose to change the way conflicts are resolved inside the system.

Perhaps the best example of this choice is how conflict-players in many jurisdictions are increasingly turning to mediation to resolve conflicts. Provided adversaries are in the mood to compromise and want to mediate, mediation has a major advantage over going to trial. Being relatively free of restrictive procedural rules that lawyers both follow and exploit, it is much less prone to gamesmanship and warrior tactics. As a result, it is usually a much less costly and quicker method of resolving conflict than going to trial. When effectively carried out, it also has the advantage of reducing hostility rather than intensifying it.

Mediation is a process in which a third party, a mediator, helps adversaries resolve a conflict by facilitating their negotiations. Mediators usually facilitate negotiations in two ways. First, they make prediction assessments based on facts and law to help the parties put an objective value on their legal claims or defences. This unbiased, third-party assessment can make it easier for the parties to reach an agreement on what the case is really worth.

Secondly, mediators adopt a problem-solving approach, looking for blockages in the bargaining process and then trying to uncover the goals and interests underlying those blockages. Mediators therefore go beyond legal objectivity and the issue of what a case is worth to develop options that might satisfy the goals and interests of both parties. Unlike a judge in a trial, the mediator has no authority to impose a judgment on the parties. The purpose of mediation is not to fix the the parties with legal responsibility, but for the parties to engage in a collaborative dialogue with the help of the mediator so that options can be jointly explored and agreement reached.

Lawyers in several jurisdictions are developing mediation advocacy skills and learning to incorporate mediation into the playing-out-conflict process. In mediation advocacy, lawyers combine advocacy and negotiation skills, ensuring they are well-prepared on facts and law, presenting both clearly for the mediator, yet also preparing themselves to work with their adversaries and the mediator to find creative solutions.

In some jurisdictions mediation is fast becoming an option lawyers regularly put to their clients. In a poll taken of American lawyers involved in mediation or arbitration hearings in the last five years, 77 per cent said clients willingly use mediation. Fifty one per cent favoured mediation over litigation for resolving disputes while only 31 per cent said they preferred litigation.[13]

As skill levels in both mediators and lawyers using mediation advocacy increase, clients and lawyers will learn to develop more trust in the process. If winning or settling to the client's satisfaction is the conflict-player's objective, mediation may soon join litigation and negotiation as a preferred method of conflict-resolution. The playing-out process would then include mediation as a typical option in the advice and decision-making stage (see Figure 6-1).

But mediation should be viewed not merely as an alternative to litigation but rather as one step in the process of solving playing-out-conflict problems. Litigation, negotiation and mediation are all part of that process. For example, proceeding initially with litigation to resolve a conflict and only later moving toward mediation has the advantage of making your adversary take the claim seriously as well as defining the issues with precision so that some future mediator can make sense of the case. If mediation does become a regular feature of the playing-out process, increasing the options for conflict-resolution, the legal system might evolve into a more just, but also more sophisticated, way of resolving conflicts.

THE VALUE OF CONFLICT BLOCKING

In the practice of law, what blockers do is less visible and controversial than what players do. As we have seen, blockers create frameworks of rules to govern future behaviour between parties.[14] They put deals together and design documents and procedures so as to anticipate conflict and prevent it. They engage in protective advocacy, negotiating or drafting terms that block conflict whether or not it actually occurs. They reduce legal and financial risk by helping clients make informed decisions and by creating greater certainty in many kinds of transactions.

Blockers are particularly important in commercial transactions because they create *comfort*. In fact, comfort is a word they use to describe assurances in letters or other documents that make clients feel legally protected. Providing comfort to clients, however, means not just providing them with the maximum legal protection to proceed with a transaction, it also increases the client's confidence and decreases uncertainty. Clients entering into commercial transactions large enough to require a lawyer's help, are invariably assuming a great deal of financial risk. A blocker can provide sufficient comfort for the client to proceed with the transaction and make risk-taking less risky. By making risk-taking more attractive, blockers undoubtedly increase people's willingness to enter into transactions, thus promoting economic activity. From an economic standpoint, the blocker's role in creating transactions is analogous to the player's role in creating court precedents. Both court precedents and well-designed transactions have a beneficial effect on future economic activity.

One of the more fascinating examples of how business lawyers have done this is in China. Although China has an irregular and incomplete legal system, Western lawyers representing clients who want to do business in China have managed to design legal structures for transactions and still provide a degree of comfort to clients investing large amounts of money in a highly risky environment.

For example, in the past 15 years lawyers have developed structures for setting up joint ventures with Chinese partners. They have designed plans to solve China-related joint-venture problems. One simple illustration in the joint-venture transaction is the design of a *letter of intent*, the letter to a prospective Chinese partner proposing a joint venture. Lawyers have learned to make the letter very flexible and to offer no concessions, particularly in relation to valuing the assets the Chinese partner is going to inject into the joint venture. The lawyers developed this letter from experience, knowing that these assets are usually overvalued by the Chinese partner and that once a concession is made on valuation or on anything else at an early stage, it is virtually impossible to reverse it.

Franklin Chu, a China-practice lawyer with Kaye Scholer, Fierman, Hays and Handler in Hong Kong pointed out that for him, China practice offered him a unique opportunity to draft laws. He regards an undeveloped system of law as a challenge and an opportunity.[15] Of course, China practice is an extreme example of how lawyers are able to structure novel types of transactions in new environments. But the development of China practice shows how conflict-blocking lawyers can break new ground, creating new law and substantial value for clients.

COMPETENCE

This final chapter takes us to the end of our search for what lawyers do. In that search, it has been useful not only to examine what they do by working from aggregate and process models, but to try to explore aspects of value in what they do. This is a critical exploration for anyone who is thinking about, or is in the process of, becoming a lawyer. Not many of us would choose to spend our professional lives doing things that have no value or meaning.

What then is the value of lawyering? For conflict players, it is resolving nagging conflicts to their clients' satisfaction, balancing winning and settling goals, but also creating precedents for others to use in a rule-of-law environment, helping them to avoid future conflict. Conflict players also have the potential to use their skills to solve the most fundamental problems of injustice in the legal system through system reform and learning new approaches to conflict-resolution.

For conflict blockers, value can be found in negotiating rules for future behaviour, blocking conflicts for clients, and reducing risk. Blockers are also responsible for creating precedents that encourage investment and economic activity. At their most creative, they have the potential to be pioneers, designing legal structures that add value to new types of transactions.

But what lawyers do has value only if they practise competently. For people at the beginning of a legal career or contemplating starting one, having the goal of doing something of value must be preceded by a more urgent goal — achieving competence. When a client who is accused of a serious crime telephones a lawyer from jail, his voice filled with anxiety, the things the lawyer needs to know immediately are how to get to the jail, what questions to ask and not to ask, and how to get him out on bail as soon as possible. Concerns about the value of what is being done are, in that situation, overshadowed by the need to focus first and foremost on avoiding mistakes.

In any consideration of the value of what lawyers do, competence must come first. Competence is not the only thing of value in law practice, but without it, nothing else matters very much. The legal profession and the courts both recognise the inherent value of competence: competence is an ethical duty[16] and gross incompetence is considered professional misconduct.[17] To clients, competence is the bottom-line requirement they demand in their legal representatives.

But what exactly is competence? This book has focused on the idea of competence as the ability to solve clients' problems because it provides a sensible framework in which to analyse what lawyers do and to understand the roles played by skills, knowledge and attitudes in solving legal problems. Academic analysis, however, cannot totally capture what competence is, though it can help people grasp many of its key elements. Competence bears the same relation to professional work as truth does to art. Like truth in art, competence in legal practice can never be definitively analysed. It is one of those qualities best described by the label "you'll know it when you see it." Though illusive, these "know-it-when-you-see-it" qualities are invariably those most worth pursuing and competence is no exception. Apart from all the value it brings to clients, competence is worth pursuing for its own sake.

[1] Ludovic Kennedy, "The Rectification of Miscarriages of Justice", (1984) *Journal of the Law Society of Scotland* (Sept.) 351–355.
[2] *State v. Sullivan* 373 P. (2d) 474 (1962).
[3] *Re Bell, ex Parte Lees* (1980) 146 C.L.R. 141.
[4] The description is based on Walter Kiechel, "The Strange Case of Kodak's Lawyers", *Fortune Magazine*, May 8, 1978, 111. See also James Stewart, *The Partners: Inside America's Most Powerful Law Firms* (Warner Books, New York, 1984).
[5] Stewart, *ibid.*, p.364.
[6] Carrie Menkel-Meadow, "Narrowing The Gap By Narrowing The Field: What's Missing From the MacCrate Report — Of Skills, Legal Science and Being A Human Being", (1994) 69 *Washington Law Review* 593–636 at 620.
[7] Walter Olson, *The Litigation Explosion: What Happened When America Unleashed the Lawsuit* (Penguin Books, Middlesex, 1992), Chap. 2.
[8] Evelle J. Younger, Attorney-General of California, *LA Times*, March 3, 1971.
[9] *Lawyers*, eds Julian Disney, Paul Redmond, John Basten and Stan Ross (The Law Book Company, NSW, 2nd ed., 1968), p.833, quoting Monroe Freedman, "Lawyers' Ethics in an Adversary System", 1975, p.2.
[10] See, generally, Ronald Coase, *The Firm, the Market and the Law* (The University of Chicago Press, Chicago, 1988), and Yoram Barzel, *Economic Analysis of Property Rights* (Cambridge University Press, Cambridge, 1989).
[11] The Right Honourable The Lord Woolf, "A New Approach To Civil Justice", Law

Lectures For Practitioners (Hong Kong Law Journal, University of Hong Kong, 1996) (forthcoming).

[12] The Right Honourable the Lord Woolf, *Access to Justice, Interim Report to the Lord Chancellor on the Civil Justice System in England and Wales*, Summary and Recommendations, June 1995, p.6.

[13] Richard C. Reuben, "The Lawyer Turns Peacemaker", (1966) (August) *ABA Journal* 54–62 at 56–7.

[14] Melvin Eisenberg, "Private Ordering Through Negotiation: Dispute-Settlement and Rulemaking", (1976) 89 *Harvard Law Review*, 637–681 at 637.

[15] Franklin Chu, "Starting Up Joint Ventures in the PRC", Asia Law and Practice Seminars, organised by Asia Law and Practice Ltd, Hong Kong, February 19, 1993.

[16] See, *e.g. The Guide to the Professional Conduct of Solicitors* (The Law Society, London, 6th ed., 1993), Chap. 12.03

[17] *Myers v. Elman* [1940] A.C. 282.

GLOSSARY

Advocacy: the ability to persuade. It is considered by many to be the most complex of the five core legal skills.

Aggregate model of competence: an analysis of competence that reveals its educational requirements.

Attitudes: dispositions or leanings that influence people to behave in a certain way.

Blocking conflict: the process of meeting client goals by minimising legal risk through preventing or blocking conflict or potential conflict.

Client interviewing and investigation: the skill of eliciting information from, and interacting with, clients to help them solve problems. Broadly defined, it includes the skill of fact investigation as well as face-to-face advising. One of the five core legal skills.

Competence: the blend of knowledge, skills and attitudes that enables lawyers to meet clients' goals or solve legal problems to their satisfaction.

Component legal skills: skills that are components (or parts) of more complex legal skills. Example:questioning is a component skill of both advocacy and negotiation.

Condition Precedent: a condition of a contract that must be met before completion, failing which the person whom the condition is meant to benefit may be released from liability to complete the contract. It is a form of escape clause.

Conflict blockers: lawyers engaged in preventing or blocking conflict to solve a legal problem.

Conflict players: lawyers engaged in playing out conflict to solve a legal problem.

Constructive trust: a trust that comes into being by operation of law when, by fraudulent, wrongful or unconscionable behaviour a person (the constructive trustee) gains legal title to property that belongs to another (the beneficiary). When a court judges that a constructive trust should be imposed on the parties and the property, it has the power to order the trustee to assign the legal title in the property to the beneficiary.

Core legal skills: five complex legal skills taught in law schools and post-LL.B professional training courses. They are commonly used by lawyers, vital to competent legal practice, and transferable to a wide variety of transactions. They include client interviewing and investigation, writing, drafting, negotiation and advocacy. As law practice evolves, other legal skills such as the skill of mediation advocacy may be added to the core.

Credible-position assessment: the lawyer's opinion of whether or not an adversary can maintain a credible position in court arguing an issue. To form an opinion the lawyer should ask, is there a rational basis for believing that the adversary has a chance of success in arguing that issue?

Deposition: in U.S. legal practice, sworn testimony given by a witness in answer to oral questions put by an attorney as part of the process of pre-trial discovery. The questions and answers are usually reduced to writing and certified as being accurately recorded. The testimony may then be used in a variety of ways at the trial. (American litigation rules provide to lawyers much wider avenues for pre-trial discovery, including the right to obtain oral testimony, than do the rules in England and many Commonwealth countries.)

Discovery: in litigation, the pre-trial process of disclosing evidence to the other side that was previously not known to it.

Drafting: the skill of creating formal documents intended to create legal relations (*e.g.* contracts) or to persuade (*e.g.* pleadings). One of the five core legal skills.

Encumbrance: an interest in land (*e.g.* a mortgage) usually evidenced by registration in an office of public record.

Escape clause: a clause in a contract that allows one or more parties to escape liability if specified events occur or do not occur.

Escrow: a method of transferring documents of title for money whereby the documents or money or both are held by a person constrained by legal duty not to release the documents or money to the parties involved until certain conditions of the escrow have been met.

Executory contract: a contract that is performed at some time later than it is made.

Flexibility: a feature of legal problem-solving characterised by the ability to modify the sequence and content of the stages of problem solving, redefine the client's goals, identify new and unforseen problems and develop creative solutions.

Generic job skills: techniques that can be used in a variety of legal and non-legal jobs.

Internal remedy: a provision in a written agreement prescribing a remedial course of action in the event of a conflict or a breach of the agreement.

Knowing the plans: knowing the details of standard procedures and documents as well as understanding the historical context in which they were developed as solutions to legal problems.

Knowledge: specific information that people are able to recall, explain or use.

Legal knowledge: specific legal information that lawyers are able to recall, explain or use.

Legal problem solving: a complex process in which the lawyer, instructed by the client, proceeds through stages overcoming obstacles to meet the client's goals.

Legal skills: techniques that lawyers know how to use in a variety of transactions or legal problems.

Linearity: a feature of legal problem-solving characterised by proceeding through a prescribed sequence of stages, or by following a prescribed plan, in order to produce a solution.

Lis pendens: a legal action that has been commenced but has not been resolved. Notice of the *lis pendens* can be registered against property in an office of public record when the property is the subject of the legal action. The property is then under the court's control until such time as it orders the *lis pendens* removed or the legal action is otherwise resolved.

Main and secondary problems: a client's main problem is what prompts the client to retain a lawyer. It is solved when a plan is successfully implemented to meet the client's goals. Secondary problems are those that arise during the process of solving the client's main problem.

Modified solution: a standard solution modified by a lawyer to meet a client's specific goals.

Negotiation: one of the five core legal skills, it is the skill of interacting with others to resolve or block conflicts.

Newly created solution: a solution to a problem not based on any standard solution known to the lawyer.

Plan: a procedure, document, solution or combination of them designed to solve a particular legal problem or category of legal problem.

Playing out conflict: the process of meeting client goals by playing out conflict in order to win or settle a case to the client's satisfaction.

Precedent: a model or standard document that lawyers use as a guide or authority when they write or draft documents or design plans for their clients. It is also a decision of a court that lawyers use as a guide or authority when advising a client on the likelihood of success of their case or when arguing the client's case in court.

Prediction assessment: the lawyer's assessment of the likelihood of success in the event a case goes to court.

Procedural law: a set of instructions explaining the methods by which rights are enforced and duties imposed.

Process model: a model or framework of action showing the steps to take or stages to pass through in order to complete the action.

Skills: techniques that people know how to use in variety of situations or problems.

Soft skills: interpersonal skills such as empathic listening or communication skills.

Substantive law: the creation, clarification and interpretation of rights that people have and duties imposed on them.

Standard document: often referred to as a precedent, it is a model document that lawyers use as a guide or authority when they write or draft documents for their clients.

Standard procedure: a model plan of step-by-step activity (*e.g.* a model checklist or body of rules) designed to solve a particular category of legal problem.

Standard solution: a model plan of step-by-step activity with accompanying documents designed to solve a particular category of legal problem. It is characterised by (1) standard procedures (*e.g.* a model checklist or body of rules); and (2) standard documents (often referred to as precedents).

Summary judgement application: an application made by one party in a legal action asking the court to grant judgment without trial. To succeed the applicant usually must show there is "no triable issue" or that the other side has "no arguable case". The application is supported by documents of record such as the pleadings as well as affidavits. In most situations witnesses may not give oral evidence.

Theory of the case: a story using law and facts designed to persuade logically and emotionally. Developing a theory of the case is central to competent advocacy.

Transaction: sometimes called a task, it is a job done by a lawyer governed by goals, procedures and rules specific to that transaction. Examples are civil litigation, criminal litigation, real-property conveyance, corporate acquisition, will.

Transactional information: all the legal information lawyers need to move successfully from the beginning to the end of a specific transaction. This includes standard procedures, standard documents and local practices for expediting them.

Transferable legal skills: legal skills that can be used in, or transferred to, a variety of different transactions.

Warranty: a representation or promise, intended by the giver to be relied on by the receiver, that something is true.

Writing: the skill of written communication. It is used to describe the creation of informal documents such as everyday correspondence, opinions, letters of advice and memoranda. One of the five core legal skills.

INDEX